**COMBAT AIRCRAFT**

**158** B-52 STRATOFORTRESS UNITS IN COMBAT 1992–2025

SERIES EDITOR TONY HOLMES

**158** | COMBAT AIRCRAFT | Peter E Davies

# B-52 STRATOFORTRESS UNITS IN COMBAT 1992–2025

OSPREY PUBLISHING

OSPREY PUBLISHING
Bloomsbury Publishing Plc
Kemp House, Chawley Park, Cumnor Hill, Oxford OX2 9PH, UK
Bloomsbury Publishing Ireland Limited,
29 Earlsfort Terrace, Dublin 2, Ireland
1385 Broadway, 5th Floor, New York, NY 10018, USA
E-mail: info@ospreypublishing.com
www.ospreypublishing.com

OSPREY is a trademark of Osprey Publishing Ltd

First published in Great Britain in 2025

© Osprey Publishing Ltd, 2025

All rights reserved. No part of this publication may be: i) reproduced or transmitted in any form, electronic or mechanical, including photocopying, recording or by means of any information storage or retrieval system without prior permission in writing from the publishers; or ii) used or reproduced in any way for the training, development or operation of artificial intelligence (AI) technologies, including generative AI technologies. The rights holders expressly reserve this publication from the text and data mining exception as per Article 4(3) of the Digital Single Market Directive (EU) 2019/790.

A catalogue record for this book is available from the British Library.

ISBN: PB 9781472865038; eBook 9781472865007; ePDF 9781472865021; XML 9781472865014

25 26 27 28 29 10 9 8 7 6 5 4 3 2 1

Edited by Tony Holmes
Cover Artwork by Gareth Hector
Aircraft Profiles and Nose Art by Jim Laurier
Index by Alan Rutter
Originated by PDQ Digital Media Solutions, UK
Printed by Repro India Ltd

Osprey Publishing supports the Woodland Trust, the UK's leading woodland conservation charity.

To find out more about our authors and books visit www.ospreypublishing.com. Here you will find extracts, author interviews, details of forthcoming events and the option to sign up for our newsletter.

**FRONT COVER**
During an OIF I mission on 11 April 2003, B-52H-170-BW 61-0021 made the first combat drop of LGBs from a Stratofortress. As 'Facet 2', commanded by Lt Col Keith Schultz and his 93rd BS/457th AEG crew, it flew from Fairford early in the morning to attack a command centre at Al Sahra airfield, north of Tikrit. A Litening II targeting pod was used by radar navigator Lt Col William Floyd to identify and designate the objective as the aircraft approached the airfield, which was defended by SA-2 and SA-8 SAMs – a challenge for electronic warfare officer Maj Trey Morris. With the aircraft flying straight and level at 30,000 ft, navigator Capt Patrick McDonald released a GBU-12D/B LGB that destroyed the objective and then used two more weapons on other targets. The B-52H also carried 16 CBU-103 dispensers, and these cluster bomb units (CBUs) were dropped on several more targets during the mission.

Like several other aircraft at the time, this B-52H carried nose art, including the slogan *"LET'S ROLL!"* beneath its cockpit on the starboard side in honour of Todd Beamer, a passenger on United Airlines Flight 93 who tried to stop terrorists that had hijacked the airliner on 11 September 2001.

The 93rd BS AFRC personnel assigned to the 457th AEW were among the most experienced in the B-52 community at the time of OIF I (*Cover Artwork by Gareth Hector*)

**PREVIOUS PAGES**
Seen here as the 23rd BS flagship, B-52H-145-BW 60-0023 flew missions in Operations *Desert Fox* and *OIF I*. The small national insignia and *USAF* lettering are barely visible on the aircraft's 4000 sq ft upper wing area (*USAF*)

# CONTENTS

**INTRODUCTION**     6

CHAPTER ONE
**DESERT STRIKE AND DESERT FOX**     14

CHAPTER TWO
**ALLIED FORCE**     23

CHAPTER THREE
**MODERN WEAPONS**     48

CHAPTER FOUR
**FREEDOM FROM TERRORISM**     55

CHAPTER FIVE
**FREE IRAQ**     71

CHAPTER SIX
**READY FOR THE FUTURE**     85

**APPENDICES**     93

COLOUR PLATES COMMENTARY     93
INDEX     96

# INTRODUCTION

In 1990 the US Air Force (USAF) still had 94 of its 102 B-52H Stratofortresses, originally delivered between May 1961 and 26 October 1962 (the same day that the final B-58A Hustler supersonic bomber was handed over by Convair), in service. Sixty-two were built with Fiscal Year (FY) 1960 funding and 40 in FY 61. In October 1962 there were 42 B-52 squadrons within Strategic Air Command (SAC) operating around 700 aircraft. Until September 1991, they provided America's very effective nuclear deterrent. At the height of the Cold War, during the 1962 Cuban Missile Crisis, B-52s completed 2000 sorties, generating 50,000 flying hours on nuclear alert within the 30 days of that potentially catastrophic confrontation with the Soviet Union.

By 2022 the active B-52 fleet had diminished through international arms reduction treaties to 76 aircraft, with 58 in active service with the 2nd Bomb Wing (BW) at Barksdale AFB, Louisiana, and the 5th BW at Minot AFB, North Dakota. A further 18 were flown by the 93rd Bomb Squadron (BS) of Air Force Reserve Command (AFRC), also at Barksdale.

From 1992 onwards the Stratofortress remained a key component in the trio of heavy, long-range bombers assigned to Air Combat Command (ACC), which, from February 2010, became Air Force Global Strike Command, and on present estimates it will continue to serve long after the other two far more recently introduced aircraft, the

The first B-52H, 60-0001 was accepted on 3 May 1961 and remains in frontline service in 2025 as *Memphis Belle IV*, attesting to the type's longevity. When the Stratofortress was being conceived, the USAF still had B-17 Flying Fortresses in service. This B-52H is unusual in having nose art on both sides of the fuselage, just like its *Belle* predecessors (*USAF*)

Rockwell B-1B Lancer and Northrop Grumman B-2A Spirit, have been withdrawn. Since 1992, the B-52 has been a key weapon in most of the conflicts which have involved American forces worldwide, despite the judgement by the USAF's Chief of Staff, Gen Merrill McPeak, in 1993 that 'the B-52 looks to me like a sunset system'. Within the US government at that time there was pressure to relegate the B-52 to second line units, but international tensions have invariably provided good reasons to keep the surviving examples on active service.

During its 70 years of operational flying, the Stratofortress has been sustained by numerous changes, updates and structural renovations. The first examples to be converted from nuclear-only capability to conventional bombing were a batch of B-52Fs in the 1964 *South Bay* programme. They went on to undertake combat roles in Vietnam, followed by B-52Ds and some B-52Gs. Project *Straight Pin* in the early 1960s strengthened the bomber's wing-to-fuselage joint, while regular re-skinning of the wings and areas of the fuselage has combated fatigue. New EFC-manufactured crash-resistant polyurethane fuel tanks were installed in B-52Hs from 2007.

The B-52H's defensive 20 mm gun armament was deleted from October 1991 to reduce costs, although the equipment associated with the weapon was retained so that it might be re-installed if necessary, as was the ejection seat in the gunner's position, which was made available for an instructor pilot. Self-protection for the bomber then became the sole responsibility of the electronic warfare officer, who monitors threats from hostile radars, jams many of them and relays the information to the pilots. This jamming capability can often be of use to protect other aircraft in a strike package. Despite having a much larger radar signature and lower speed than the B-1B, with which it has often operated in recent conflicts, the B-52H is still viable as a carrier of varied 70,000-lb weapons loads over long distances.

Alongside many updates and improvements, in 2006 B-52Hs still had the 'legacy' cockpit controls for the AGM-28 Hound Dog stand-off air-to-ground missiles that had been carried throughout the Cold War and fittings for the partial pressure suits once required for very high-altitude flight. The B-52Gs' underwing stub weapons pylons, designed for Hound Dog missiles, were transferred to B-52Hs during the Conventional Enhancement Modification (CEM) programme that allowed the nuclear

H-model Stratofortresses continued to undertake SAC's nuclear deterrent Single Integrated Operational Plan (SIOP) mission, initially in silver and white colours as seen here on B-52H-135-BW 60-0002 of the 719th BS/449th BW. The unit called Kincheloe, Michigan, AFB home, with this particular aircraft being based there from 1963 to 1973 (*USAF*)

B-52H force to take over the conventional role. The original B-52G I-beam weapons rack adapter was replaced by the heavy stores adaptation beam (HSAB), a single example of which could hold nine Mk 82s, M117s or CBUs. CEM also meant the aircraft could carry precision guided weapons (PGMs). The first conversion, using considerable quantities of wiring from a retired B-52G, was completed on 23 September 1993.

The overall Gunship Gray paint scheme seen on virtually all 21st century B-52Hs was preceded by SIOP camouflage, a faded example of which is seen here. The 319th BW from Grand Forks AFB, North Dakota, sent two H-models to RAF Marham, Norfolk, in 1981 for the *Great Strike* bombing competition. B-52H-145-BW 60-0026 and B-52H-170-BW 61-0022 displayed 'Yosemite Sam' tail artwork. Older B-52Ds also continued to visit RAF bases for NATO *Busy Brewer/Priory* exercises during this period (*Author's Collection*)

Ninety-eight B-52Gs were converted to carry the AGM-86B air-launched cruise missile (ALCM) with a W-80 nuclear warhead, and 57 were reallocated from 1988 to conventional bombing. As the G-models were retired between 1992–94, the B-52H and B-1B took over their conventional bombing role when SAC was combined with ACC in 1992 as Cold War tensions subsided.

In the mid-1990s the nuclear role passed to the 509th BW and its 21 B-2A Spirit 'stealth' bombers. The B-52Hs' conventional weapons capability was enhanced beyond CEM, which had benefited 66 aircraft by 1999. Eight examples were modified in the 1994 *Rapid Eight* programme to provide some capability with PGMs while the CEM programme was still a year away. Four were given AGM-84 Harpoon anti-shipping missile capability and four more were equipped to carry the AGM-142 Have Nap stand-off missile.

B-52Hs still retained basic nuclear delivery ability, but from September 2015 the New Strategic Arms Reduction Treaty (New START) required the reduction of nuclear-capable bombers to just 60 – 19 B-2As and 41 B-52Hs. The rest of the B-52H fleet was modified for non-nuclear deliveries, including 12 aircraft in desert storage that had their nuclear delivery equipment removed. B-1Bs, which had lost their nuclear wiring and fusing systems in the mid-1990s, had further modifications to remove any nuclear weapons carrying capability.

In 2017 Barksdale AFB received updates to facilitate reversion to nuclear configuration in case its B-52Hs would ever be required to go back on Cold War nuclear alert, but it was made clear that this was not planned. In fact, when a B-52H flew to Barksdale from Minot in August 2007 mistakenly loaded with ALCMs complete with their nuclear warheads, the 'fallout' brought about the resignations of the Secretary of the Air Force and the Chief of Staff of the Air Force.

After the remaining 30 B-52Hs in service, together with 12 in storage, were converted for conventional bombing only, it was considered necessary to maintain a strategic reserve of aircraft, rotating them through active squadrons to stretch the fatigue life of the Stratofortress fleet. This was costing the US taxpayer $75m annually in 2001. In 2008 the USAF defeated a Pentagon attempt to reduce the B-52H force to 56, and it has remained at around 76 since then.

## COMBAT CONFIGURATION

The B-52H's two standard weapons bays can each hold two four-weapon CBU racks or three nine-weapon clip-in racks. The requirements of a series of major combat engagements worldwide have coincided with the evolutionary expansion of the B-52H's armoury and the aircraft's range of bomb-carrying options, both internal and on its wing pylons.

While conventional 'dumb' bombs were the primary armament for the conflicts of the 1980s and early 1990s, the B-52H was gradually re-fitted to handle a wide selection of Global Positioning System (GPS) or laser-guided bombs, modified from conventional 500- and 2000-lb weapons as Joint Direct Attack Munitions (JDAM). The 1760 Internal Weapons Bay Upgrade, installed in the bomb-bay area, introduced the carriage of PGMs such as the GBU-12 internally, modifying the common strategic rotary launcher (CSRL), which acts as a rotating weapons release rack, into a conventional rotary launcher (CRL) by 2016. It was then able to hold JDAM, the AGM-158 Joint Air-to-Surface Standoff Missile (JASSM) or miniature air-launched decoys. In effect, CRL increased the B-52H's smart weapons capacity by around 50 per cent, and aircraft with the system deployed for the first time in November 2017 when the 69th Expeditionary Bomb Squadron (EBS) flew to Al Udeid, in Qatar, for combat duties.

Carrying many of the weapons internally could free up the wings to increase range, although GBU-31 LGBs have sometimes been carried externally in place of JDAM or ALCMs. The CIBR2 upgrade also allowed B-52H navigators to reprogramme Conventional Air Launched Cruise Missiles (CALCM) in flight. JASSM had replaced the AGM-86C/D CALCM (an AGM-86 with a conventional warhead), used extensively in B-52H operations, by November 2019, although the nuclear AGM-86B, in use since 1981, was retained. New external pylons, included in the 2019 Bomber Vector programme, will quadruple the weight of ordnance that they can carry to 40,000 lbs.

Updating the B-52H's weapons systems to cope with successive new generations of missiles and other ordnance that it is expected to carry has been a long process, starting with the original early 1960s analogue AN/ASQ-38 bomb/navigation system. By the 1970s the latter was clearly unable to manage the ALCMs, which were foreseen as the B-52's principal weapon. The AN/ASQ-38 was replaced by the digital AN/ASQ-176 Offensive Avionics System, similar to the equipment developed for the B-1A. B-52Hs had been retrofitted by 1986. GPS equipment was added shortly afterwards. However, ten years later, the increasing demands on the AN/ASQ-176 and a shortage of spare parts necessitated a major update in lieu of costly replacement of the aircraft.

More recently, the Litening II and Sniper lightweight targeting pods have allowed the B-52H to target and launch its own PGMs. The pods soon became more frequently used for targeting than the B-52G/H's two 'chin' turrets. The latter contained an AN/AAQ-6 forward looking infra-red (FLIR) sensor and an AN/AVQ-22 steerable low light level television as components of the ASQ-151 electro-optical viewing system (EVS), retro-fitted to B-52Hs from 1972. EVS data was presented on the navigators' and pilots' ten-inch cockpit screens, providing terrain avoidance imagery, time-to-go before weapons release and overall information on altitude, speed, attitude and position. The system was designed with surface-to-air missile (SAM)-avoiding low-altitude nuclear attack in mind, but by 2005 the B-52Hs were flying few such sorties. Targeting pods also offered a zoom option for a closer, high fidelity look at the target.

## NATURE OF THE BEAST

Despite the ongoing modernisation of the B-52 fleet, the veteran aircraft's essential nature as an early 1950s heavy bomber remains in many respects, and the cockpit looks much as it did in the 1970s. Trainee pilots quickly learned that flying it through mechanical control runs involved considerable 'inertia management' and some gym work on the muscles to build up enough strength to handle this pre-fly-by-wire aircraft.

After moving the control yoke to initiate a banking movement, there would be an appreciable pause before anything happened. The B-52H's tendency towards Dutch roll made it a challenge to hold steady on the tanker during a typical 20-minute in-flight refuelling session. Having only spoilers rather than ailerons for wing control requires some adjustment for trainee pilots coming from basic training.

At maximum low-altitude speeds (around 460 mph) the nose tended to dip down due to 'Mach tuck', requiring careful trimming by the pilot. However, the aircraft has proved to be remarkably resilient, as seen on 8 August 1995 when 2nd BW B-52H 60-0054 shed its entire port inboard pylon and both attached engines but managed to land safely at Barksdale.

The B-52 has often been regarded as a 'navigator's aeroplane', in which the pilots just react to instructions from the two navigators in the lightless lower deck 'pit'. Increasingly sophisticated avionics and weapons systems have only served to enhance the importance of this 'offense team'. In the left-hand seat, the radar navigator is principally occupied with managing the weapons systems, while the right-hand navigator, usually with less experience than the radar navigator, concentrates on timing and routes. However, both officers work closely together during weapons delivery.

Although the B-52H fleet has ranged worldwide in its assignments to conflict situations, it has remained at two homeland bases since the inactivation of four B-52H wings in 1993–95. The 410th BW at K I Sawyer AFB, Michigan, had been an early H-model operator in 1963, but it was inactivated in November 1994. At Griffiss AFB, New York, the 416th BW converted to B-52Hs from G-models in 1992, only to close down two years later. The 7th BW at Carswell AFB, Texas, had H-models among other B-52 variants from 1983 until December 1992. Finally, the 92nd BW at Fairchild AFB, Washington, which had been a B-52 operator since 1957, had surrendered its H-models by May 1994.

Budget cuts in 1996 forced a reduction in operational B-52Hs to only 66 aircraft, with 16 being retired. Bombers from the inactivated units went to the enlarged 2nd BW at Barksdale or the 5th BW at Minot, with both wings controlled by the Eighth Air Force headquartered at the 22,000-acre Barksdale base. Minot, as the more northerly base, has climatic limitations including severe sub-zero temperatures, poor visibility and

Although, as an associate unit, the 11th BS no longer operates its own aircraft, B-52H-135-BW 60-0011 retains its flagship markings and historic 'Mr Jiggs' nose art denoting the bomber's assignment to the squadron CO – then Lt Col Daniel A Kosin. From 2009 the 11th shared the B-52 training programme with the AFRC's 93rd BS, using aircraft from the latter unit (*USAF*)

winds gusting at 40–50 mph, while Barksdale experiences the heat and humidity of Louisiana, but offers better operating conditions.

Equipped with B-52s since April 1963, the 2nd BW moved to Barksdale from Hunter AFB, Georgia, and became a B-52 'super wing'. In 1994 it acquired the 11th BS, which traced its origins as far back as 1917. The unit served as the B-52H training squadron until 2009, when it shared that responsibility with the AFRC's 93rd BS, which supplied the aircraft for that purpose. The 20th BS, which moved to Barksdale from Carswell AFB in 1992 following nine years flying B-52Hs from Texas, had a similarly long history as a bomber squadron. Once assigned to the 2nd BW, it took responsibility for operational development of the AGM-142 Have Nap missile.

The 2nd BW's 96th BS also has a long heritage including bombing operations in both World Wars, followed by 30 years of inactivation. Revived as a B-52H unit within the 2nd Operations Group (OG) at Barksdale in October 1993, it replaced the 596th BS. The 96th took on operational use of the AGM-84 Harpoon and AGM-86C CALCM. It became better known for a record 47.2 hours around-the-world flight in August 1994. Two aircraft – 60-0008 and 60-0059, commanded by Brig Gen George P Cole and Col James A Hawkins, respectively – completed Exercise *Global Power 94-7*, which included an overflight of the Udairi Range Complex in Kuwait, where they delivered Mk 82 bombs after 17 hours in flight. It was an impressive precursor of the long-range missions that the squadron would fly two years later in Operation *Desert Strike*.

Barksdale also hosted the 917th Wing, formerly a fighter unit, which became a Composite Wing in 1993 for its 93rd BS to manage training on the B-52H and also to deploy for operations abroad. A long-standing unit tracing its ancestry back to the 93rd Aero Squadron of 1918, the 93rd BS was also reactivated in 1993 after a 30-year hiatus and duly became the first AFRC B-52 squadron. B-52H 60-0045, delivered by Col William Brooks, was the first heavy bomber to join an AFRC unit. Emphasising its global posture, the 93rd sent three aircraft to RAF Fairford, in Gloucestershire, on 26 April 1996 to acclimatise crews to three days of 'bare base' operations. Four B-52Hs and five B-1Bs repeated the visit less than two months later.

The 917th Wing was redesignated the 307th BW/OG of the Tenth Air Force, AFRC, in January 2011. The wing retained the 93rd BS, which continued to provide crew training. From 2009 all students received a seven-month course in both nuclear and conventional combat flying – annually, around 24 crews usually completed B-52H qualification training. As part of the Total Force Enterprise (TFE) concept that brought active and reserve components together at Barksdale from 2009, the 307th BW was also linked to the 7th BW and its B-1B Lancers at Dyess AFB, Texas. The same year that TFE commenced, the 93rd BS had 18 B-52Hs on strength, and it joined other active-duty Stratofortress units in participating in the nuclear deterrent role. The 93rd also became the first B-52 unit to qualify in the use of the Rafael/Northrop Grumman AN/AAQ-28(V) Litening II AT targeting pod, incorporating it into H-model combat tactics during Operation *Iraqi Freedom I* (OIF I) in 2003.

The 96th BS's flagship, 60-0059, features the unit's long-lived insignia designed by Harry O Lawson in 1917 at the start of an operational history that continued virtually uninterrupted until 1963. Thirty years later, the squadron was reactivated as part of the 2nd OG, pioneering the use of the AGM-84 Harpoon and AGM-86C CALCM (*Author's Collection*)

The 307th OG also contains the 343rd BS at Barksdale, re-activated in 2010 and deploying worldwide for contingency missions within Global Strike Command. Originally formed at Barksdale in 1942 as a B-24 Liberator squadron, it participated in many crucial operations including the Ploiesti oil refinery attacks and B-29 raids on Japan. Post-war, the unit replaced its Superfortresses with B-47 Stratojets in 1954 and was eventually inactivated in 1966.

Over the years, Barksdale has also lent B-52Hs to the 340th Weapons Squadron, a detached unit of the 57th Wing at Nellis AFB, Nevada, that specialises in tactics and weapons training. Finally, two aircraft (including 60-0049) at Barksdale sported 'OT' tail codes indicating their ownership by the 49th Test and Evaluation Squadron (TES), part of the 53rd Wing at Eglin AFB, Florida, for whom they conducted evaluation of the B-52H and its weapons systems.

At Minot AFB, the 5th BW operated two B-52H units from 1995. The wing's motto 'Kiai O Ka Lewa' derives from its origins in 1919 at Luke Field, Hawaii, where the 5th Bombardment Group remained until 1942. After extensive service in the Far East in World War 2, it flew RB/B-36 Peacemakers before receiving SAC's first batch of B-52Gs in 1959 at Travis AFB, California. Inactivated in 1968, the 5th was transferred 'on paper' to Minot in view of its long heritage, replacing the 405th BW and inheriting its B-52Hs for the wing's sole squadron at that time, the 23rd BS, another unit with origins stretching back to 1917.

Minot briefly operated a second unit, the 72nd BS, from 6 January 1995 to 1 July 1996, absorbing B-52Hs from the inactivated 410th and 416th BWs. On 3 September 2009 this unit was finally replaced by the 69th BS, another former B-36 operator. Since 1956, the unit's B-52s have made many foreign deployments, including those for Vietnam operations and later in Operation *Desert Storm* with the 42nd BW from Loring AFB, Maine. It has also deployed aircraft to Andersen AFB, Guam, in 2010 and to Fairford (which its B-52Gs had often visited during Gulf operations) for NATO exercises. The 69th returned to Fairford on a two-month expeditionary deployment in April 2022.

Fluctuations in the size of the B-52 fleet continued during the 1990s as US Department of Defense (DoD) policies varied. In the FY 1995 budget B-52Hs with a history of wing cracks and fuel leaks were withdrawn and ACC proposed to keep only 47 for two active wings, with some allocated to the AFRC and 20 put in storage to be 'regenerated' as necessary.

In May 1997 policy changes saw the B-52H quota re-set at 71, together with 95 B-1Bs and 21 B-2As. Following the subsequent crash of two B-1Bs, a further five B-52Hs were added from the 'retired' reserve stock, but only 44 were regarded as being available for potential combat. By mid-2001 all bar 14 aircraft had been converted with the CSRL, which could take eight AGM-86B/C ALCMs or B61 and B83 nuclear stores. Eight had AGM-142 Have Nap missile capability and a few had AGM-129 Advanced Cruise Missile (ACM) launch equipment. By 2005 numbers had settled at 86, but three more were lost in accidents between 2008 and 2016.

A Fiscal Year 2019 budget announcement included funding for 75 B-52Hs until at least 2050 and a $22 billion upgrade package including the aim to fit new engines. As part of the same plan, the B-2A and B-1B are scheduled to retire early when the Northrop Grumman B-21 Raider stealth bomber enters service. The B-52H's much lower operating costs were a major factor in this decision. In 2016 they were quoted as $69,708 per flying hour, compared with $169,313 for the B-2A Spirit. However, the overall mission-capable rate for all three bomber types at the time was only about 50 per cent.

## SPANNING THE WORLD

From 4 August 1998 the USAF established ten Air Expeditionary Forces (AEFs), each with around 175 fixed wing aircraft and helicopters, to deploy rapidly to trouble spots around the world. They were each intended to deploy for a maximum of 120 days, reducing longer foreign commitments. A typical AEF had six B-52Hs or B-1Bs temporarily allocated to it, together with fighters, A-10A/Cs and tankers.

The 2nd AEF was regularly assigned to Andersen AFB, from where it flew *Global Power* missions, taking its aircraft as far as South Korea, Wake Island and Japan, among many other destinations. In the early 2000s each squadron was required to complete four long-ranging *Global Power* missions annually. These flights could take at least 18 hours, and included simulated weapons delivery within the tasking typically undertaken by the AEF.

Some were 'round robin' missions, returning to base at the end, but they could also include overseas deployment with all the attendant logistics issues. The longer flights required an extra relief pilot and navigator. A typical mission allowed for two simulated target runs, usually over bombing ranges, between long periods of high-altitude cruising, often crossing several time zones, with consequences for a crew's circadian rhythms and sleep patterns. The B-52H's range enabled crews in mid-2001 to take off from Minot AFB, cross the Atlantic and run simulated attacks on an electronic warfare range in Denmark. They then returned to North Dakota with tanker support from the 100th ARW at RAF Mildenhall, in Suffolk.

The combat operations flown by the B-52H force from 1992 to the present have required plenty of that adaptability, exceptionally long-range flying and the ability to operate within an integrated strike force.

# CHAPTER ONE

# DESERT STRIKE AND DESERT FOX

B-52H operations in the Middle East from 1996 to date have been grounded in the experience of crews who flew the B-52G in Operation *Desert Storm* (see *Osprey Combat Aircraft 50 – B-52 Stratofortress Units in Operation Desert Storm* for further details). For Stratofortress units, the 1991 Gulf War opened with the take-off of seven B-52Gs from Barksdale AFB at 0636 hrs on 16 January for the first strikes in an air operation that would last for 38 days. During the longest combat mission ever flown up to that time, crews fired AGM-86C CALCMs at Iraqi communications hubs and electrical supply sources. Shortly after those missiles left their B-52G launch platforms, AGM-114 Hellfire missiles from US helicopters destroyed Iraqi early-warning radar sites, opening the way for an unprecedented aerial onslaught that effectively neutralised the majority of Iraq's complex and extremely expensive defences within two days.

Diego Garcia-based B-52Gs of the 4300th BW (Provisional) were tasked with hitting five Iraqi Air Force (IrAF) forward-deployment airfields 15 miles from the Saudi Arabian border. Cockpit lights were taped over and green chemical light sticks were used to assist the night-vision goggles worn for low-altitude attacks.

In the foreground is B-52H-155-BW 60-0054 *MUD BUFF*, which was flown by Lt Col Floyd L Carpenter during *Desert Strike* on 2 September 1996. Twenty-seven years later, in March–July 2023, the bomber deployed to Guam on a BTF assignment, training with other regional nationalities including aircraft of the Republic of China Air Force (*USAF*)

The bombers flew in trail formation with 500 ft vertical separation. Formations of three B-52Gs, with air spares, were assigned to each airfield, with two aircraft dropping British 1000-lb bombs to crater runways and one B-52 laying down 51 CBU canisters to impede subsequent repairs. The CBU-delivering bomber had to climb to 1000 ft to drop, exposing it to more air defence opposition, while the aircraft dropping 'UK thousand pounders' crossed the target at 500 ft.

All of the Stratofortresses needed two inflight refuelling sessions en route to the target area. In all, 17 KC-135 tankers were required.

Approaching the target area, the B-52s dropped to lower altitude, flying in single-line 'bomber stream' formation six miles apart at 345–575 mph to avoid Iraqi radars. The trio of jets would then separate to make their attacks from three different directions, hitting it 45 seconds apart. Follow-up passes by F-15E Strike Eagles were usually part of the attacking package. The mission would then end at an airfield in Saudi Arabia, where the B-52s were checked for combat damage and (in 1991) contamination by chemical or biological weapons.

The Iraqi defences were taken seriously, and crews wore survival gear, sidearms and, in some cases, flak vests. At low attitude there was plenty of 23 mm and 37 mm gunfire to contend with, and pilots often had to 'jink' as far as is possible in a bomber with a 185 ft wingspan. This type of mission profile was continued over the first three nights of *Desert Storm*, and was often used in modified forms for later B-52 operations over Iraq and Afghanistan.

A relatively small number of PGMs were used in accordance with the US doctrine of 'surgical strikes' to neutralise key targets with a minimum of collateral damage. However, in the primary objective of driving President Saddam Hussein's army out of Kuwait, which occupied three-quarters of the Coalition air effort, battlefield interdiction, including heavy bombing, was a far greater contributor than close air support (CAS). In 42,240 sorties, US aircraft delivered mainly 'dumb' bombs, including 43,435 M117 750-lb bombs dropped by B-52Gs. Strategic sorties included 1500 against command-and-control facilities and 970 against nuclear, chemical and biological warfare targets, although most of the latter were failures.

In the wake of *Desert Storm*, Operation *Desert Calm* saw half-a-million US troops and the USAF's Ninth Air Force returned to the USA. However, Saddam Hussein's persecution of the Kurds in northern Iraq soon began, and

When extended, all 797 sq ft of the B-52H's trailing edge Fowler-type flaps initially rotate downwards and then move rearwards, powered by two 53-ampere motors. Extension and retraction each take one minute. Slots for eight chaff dispensers are located between the flap segments (*USAF*)

Operation *Provide Comfort* was instigated to protect Kurdish territory. *Desert Storm* was followed by a period in which no-fly zones (NFZs) were imposed in Operations *Southern Watch* and *Northern Watch* after Iraq fired missiles and AAA at Coalition aircraft more than 150 times. This cat-and-mouse suppression of enemy air defences (SEAD) operation continued for the best part of a decade, with the final attacks on aircraft in the southern NFZ occurring on the eve of OIF I in March 2003.

For October 1994's Operation *Vigilant Warrior*, six 5th BW B-52Hs were among 170 Allied aircraft available to support 100,000 troops in opposing Iraq's renewed build-up of forces on the Kuwaiti border. A combat air support shield was maintained across the northern part of Kuwait, frustrating Iraq's desire to begin a second invasion of the country.

In 1996 Coalition opposition became more determined, with a cruise missile attack on Iraqi air defence sites in Operation *Desert Strike* on 3 September in direct response to Saddam Hussein's opportunist incursion into Kurdish lands where rival factions were in conflict. Iraqi forces sided with the pro-Baghdad faction and began to massacre the opposition Kurdish elements, effectively ending the long-running *Provide Comfort*.

Maj Gen Floyd L Carpenter, who, as a lieutenant colonel, led the *Desert Strike* mission, assumed command of the Eighth Air Force on 1 June 2009 and retired in 2011 after 33 years of service (*USAF*)

The September 1996 attacks on Iraq included the active combat debut of the B-52H. Defying United Nations' (UN) resolutions and the Coalition forces' efforts to protect Iraqis living in the northern part of the country in *Provide Comfort*, Saddam Hussein had sent three divisions of his Republican Guard to attack the Kurdish city of Erbil on 31 August. Less than 20 hours later, Lt Col Floyd L Carpenter, leading the 96th BS/2nd BW deployment, was told to prepare for three of the unit's aircraft, including one air spare, to hit targets in southern Iraq with AGM-86C CALCMs. Lt Col Carpenter explained to the author that deciding the route when planning the mission at Barksdale was his first challenge;

'Lt Gen [Phillip J] Ford, commander of the Eighth Air Force, made it clear that we would have to fly west. Diplomatic clearance would not be granted to fly an easterly route or launch missiles that would require flying over foreign soil, except Iraq. We had decided to deploy four aircraft, although it was fairly certain that only two would fly the mission. Eventually, six were loaded with weapons, although only four went to Guam. Take-off was to be made at around 1700 hrs. En route to Guam was 15.8 hrs, with two air refuellings, the first just off the west coast and the second around Hawaii. Arrival at Guam was at midnight, and at 0400 hrs the next morning [1 September] we made it to our rooms to sleep.'

By then Lt Col Carpenter had been awake since the morning of 30 August;

'Three aircraft were to take off [from Guam as part of *Desert Strike*], with the best two continuing to launch missiles. We did minimal route and target study before proceeding to the aircraft, and we launched at 1900 hrs on 2 September, 19 hours after landing at Guam. Our first refuelling was with five KC-135Rs, and immediately afterwards the third [air spare] B-52H with Capt Bill Bilton in command turned back to Guam.'

Two B-52Hs (60-0054 'Duke 01', commanded by Lt Col Carpenter, and 60-0014 'Duke 02', manned by Capt Parker Northrup III and his crew) continued on. According to Carpenter;

'The second refuelling, sharing the offloads of one KC-10 – the other had become unserviceable – put us behind our required fuel plan. For that reason, when two more KC-10s showed up to refuel us south of the Persian Gulf, I decided to take on as much as possible, and both aircraft refuelled above the 448,000 lbs maximum inflight weight. As we approached the Strait of Hormuz, we began receiving radio calls asking for identification. We gave the standard response of a US aircraft on a routine training mission. These radio calls persisted, warning us that we were nearing a firing zone. Eventually, two Mirage interceptors were launched and gave chase.'

The pair of IrAF Mirage F1EQs were driven off by escorting F-14Ds from VF-11 and VF-31, embarked in USS *Carl Vinson* (CVN-70). Warships from the carrier's battle group would also fire 43 RGM/UGM-109 Tomahawk Land Attack Missiles (TLAMs) as part of *Desert Strike*.

Carpenter continued;

'The flight up to this point had been fairly routine, although with a voice satellite radio on board we were getting inputs from Barksdale, Guam and CENTCOM [US Central Command], which made for more confusion than anything. Although this radio made it possible to receive updates to target priorities, offering greater flexibility, it also created problems.

'As we prepared to launch missiles, the navigators had realised that the assigned targets now resided on two different mission tapes, meaning that we would have to reboot the system in the middle of the launch – this required an extra three minutes while the system "timed out". As we approached the southern coast of Kuwait, we separated our formation and began launching missiles. Our first three launches were uneventful, and then we had to change tapes, resulting in the missiles not being ready for launch before reaching the end of our "launch box". We had to turn back, having only launched half our loads. There was complete silence and dejection in the aircraft and at Eighth Air Force HQ too, as our EWO [electronic warfare officer] had already radioed back our launch issues.

'Sitting in the IP [instructor pilot] seat, I casually mentioned that we should turn around and launch the rest of our missiles, as they were now "timed out" and ready to go. A cheer went up, and as the EWO radioed back our intentions, the pilot continued his turn back to the bomb-run heading and we launched the remainder of our CALCMs. My aircraft launched six and the other B-52 launched seven. We then reversed our course and headed back out of the Gulf, with our Navy escort still in place – those guys did a great job for us. Exiting the Gulf, we received the same threatening phone calls, and [IrAF Mirage F1EQ] interceptors were launched again, but they never got within 40 miles of our position.

'Because we had taken on so much gas, we still had plenty to recover to Diego Garcia [in the Indian Ocean] without air refuelling. So when a KC-10 showed up with 180,000 lbs of available fuel, I instructed my wingman to take the entire offload and proceed on to Guam, where the majority of our maintenance personnel and supplies were still located. Shortly after we had separated the formation, another KC-10 from Diego Garcia arrived with another 180,000 lbs. I took the entire offload and headed for Guam myself.

'As we neared Thailand, the weather turned very bad, with thunderstorms everywhere, and there were moments when I questioned the wisdom of my decision as our fuel began to dwindle. It turned out I had nothing to worry about as this airplane seems to "make" gas as it gets lighter and altitude is increased accordingly. We dodged thunderstorms around Vietnam and even talked to some commercial airliners who congratulated us for the mission – I assume they had already heard about it on the news. When we arrived back we did simultaneous approaches on the parallel runways at Andersen AFB, touching down together at dawn – the closest thing to a formation landing a B-52 can do. Everyone was out to meet us, maintenance personnel and officers in formation, saluting us as we taxied in. Although we were tired from the 33.9 hours, 13,600 miles trip, everyone was excited about the successful mission.'

Operation *Desert Thunder* included the combat debut of the B-1B, which became a regular partner for the B-52H in subsequent operations, including *Desert Fox*. B-1B 85-0064, assigned to Col Greg Gardner, commanding the Kansas ANG's 184th BW, is seen here with B-52H-135-BW 60-0003 of the 93rd BS/917th BW in 1997 (*Author*)

A Baghdad power station and communications centres were hit by the CALCMs, which also struck air defence sites and command centres. 'Duke 02' had problems with its electronic countermeasures (ECM), which might have assisted the enemy defences, but 'Duke 01's' equipment and the attendant Tomcats compensated for the faults. In the wake of this operation, the two 96th BS crews shared the MacKay Trophy, which is awarded annually by the USAF for the 'most meritorious flight of the year'.

Following these strikes, the 96th BS group divided, with two B-52Hs and support crews transferring to Diego Garcia, where they were joined by two more Stratofortresses. Meanwhile, the pair of B-52Hs still at Andersen AFB returned to Barksdale, where they were joined by the four Diego Garcia bombers by 12 October 1996 when no further strikes where authorised. The use of CALCMs had been generally successful, although at least three failed to reach their target, two of them being seen to crash into the Persian Gulf.

Despite *Desert Strike*, Saddam Hussein's intransigence showed no signs of abating. In November 1997 he demanded that Americans participating in the UN Special Commission (UNSCOM) inspection teams searching for Iraq's weapons of mass destruction (WMD) should leave Iraq. President Bill Clinton responded by despatching eight Barksdale B-52Hs to Diego Garcia on 19 November. As tensions continued into 1998, six more 2nd BW aircraft joined the deployment. The anticipated deterrent effect on the Iraqi leaders calmed their rhetoric, and the B-52Hs were able to return to Louisiana by mid-June.

However, the situation soon deteriorated again, and Saddam Hussein continued to refuse compliance with the UNSCOM requirements. The 2nd BW sent seven aircraft to Diego Garcia from 14 November, together with five 5th BW examples, for the planned Operation *Desert Thunder* – these aircraft were assigned to the 2nd Air Expeditionary Group (AEG), commanded by Col Robert A Bruley. If *Desert Thunder* had been initiated, it would have seen the combat debut of the B-1B Lancer, for 28th BW aircraft from Ellsworth AFB, South Dakota, had deployed to Bahrain. Despite further sudden, mercurial changes of policy by Saddam Hussein, he finally allowed UN inspectors limited access to alleged WMD sites, and *Desert Thunder* was called off. However, his obstructive attitude was soon resumed, and on 11 December the 2nd BW's Diego Garcia contingent was joined by seven Minot-based B-52Hs. Five days later, the brief Operation *Desert Fox* began.

## DESERT FOX

*Desert Thunder* had been conceived as a punitive response to Saddam Hussein's continued obstruction of UN inspection of his suspected WMD sites. It also responded to his attempts to shoot down US reconnaissance aircraft, including Lockheed U-2Rs. Although their numbers had been greatly reduced, the presence of SA-2 and SA-6 SAMs, among others, was a persistent threat to Allied air superiority. For B-52 crews, the SA-2 threat was one with a long history dating back to the Vietnam War, but the missile was still potentially effective despite its age. The response from the planners' perspective had been suppression rather than destruction of the elusive SAM sites.

In November 1997, Saddam Hussein had ordered the UNSCOM inspectors to leave Iraq, leading to a build-up of US forces for potential responses, including an increase in the number of 2nd BW B-52Hs at Diego Garcia to eight aircraft. Diplomacy calmed the situation and the bombers returned to Barksdale in June.

The Iraqis' non-cooperation increased, and by November 1998 UN patience was exhausted. The UNSCOM team was duly advised to leave to avoid punitive Coalition military action. As the team left, they estimated that 32,000 chemical munitions, 550 mustard gas bombs and 4000 tons of related chemical substances remained undiscovered. The build-up of US and British forces continued, including seven 2nd BW B-52Hs for the 96th EBS under Col Wendell Griffin at Diego Garcia.

Several of these aircraft headed for Iraq on 14 November, and they were about 15 minutes away from their CALCM launch point as part of Operation *Desert Thunder* (originally codenamed *Desert Viper*) when Saddam Hussein suddenly restored permission for the inspection to continue. The B-52s were recalled, and a much larger wave of strikes by carrier-based US Navy aircraft and other USAF types, as well as ship-launched cruise missiles, was halted at the request of UN Secretary General, Kofi Annan. Even so, American determination was made clear by the reinforcement of the Diego Garcia bomber force on 11 December by seven 23rd BS B-52Hs and eight from Barksdale.

International frustration with the Iraqi regime soon found expression in Operation *Desert Fox*, conducted from 16–19 December, which, in Secretary of State Madeleine Albright's opinion, was aimed at 'degrading his ability to use weapons of mass destruction'.

On the 16th, Saddam Hussein's intelligence network advised him that no Coalition aircraft were in the area. No B-52s were inbound and the US Navy had only one carrier – USS *Enterprise* (CVN-65) – on station with Fifth Fleet. They also noted that President Clinton was involved in an impeachment trial and that the Muslim fasting period of Ramadan was due to start on the 20th, considerably reducing the chances of politically unacceptable US action. The Iraqi president therefore assumed that he could continue to defy the UN with impunity. In the opinion of his

Deputy Prime Minister, Tariq Aziz, 'The reality is that the resources they [the Allies] could assemble for this aggression are limited. They cannot throw missiles every day for a whole month'.

However, following a barrage of 250 cruise missiles from US Navy ships that night, which preceded a 33-aircraft strike mounted by Carrier Air Wing Three from *Enterprise*, the B-52Hs weighed in the following night (17 December) with 12 aircraft in two flights, with two air spares. The first flight was manned by crews from the 96th BS as 'Ruben 11–17' (including 60-0016), the aircraft being led by the squadron commander, Maj Keith Anderson. The second flight attacked six hours later, with 23rd BS crews as 'Blade 21–27' (including 61-0023 and five others) being led by Lt Col Douglas Haynor, CO of the 23rd BS. Each bomber carried eight AGM-86 Block 1 CALCMs internally, these weapons featuring 3000-lb warheads and much improved GPS systems. The force refuelled from KC-10As en route and fired 74 missiles successfully at Iraq's Ministries of Defence and six of the president's palaces.

A final punch on the 17th came from an evening mission flown by two B-52Hs crewed by personnel from both the 20th and 96th BSs, firing another salvo of 16 CALCMs. This two-ship mission was notable for the inclusion of 1Lt Cheryl Lamoureux of the 20th BS, who became the first woman ever to participate in a USAF combat mission.

Weapons and research sites for WMD were targeted, as well as air defence installations, eight Republican Guard HQs (to weaken Saddam Hussein's control), Ba'ath Party palaces and an oil refinery in Basra – the latter was hit by a pair of B-1B Lancers to end Iraq's illegal oil exports. Missile fabrication facilities were destroyed at both the Ibn al Haytham missile research and design centre and the large Taji plant, where SA-2 and SA-3 SAMs and control radars were repaired, causing severe damage to three buildings.

The latter factory was also developing the technology for long-range ballistic missiles that could have carried Iraq's WMD warheads to foreign targets. Some of the country's remaining Scud-B ballistic missiles, disassembled so as to be hidden, were also destroyed, although many more were still thought to be secreted away throughout Iraq. Finally, early warning radars and 34 air defence facilities were also eliminated, opening up the target areas for B-52H attacks the following night.

By 22 November the Stratofortresses were able to redeploy to the USA, although four remained at Diego Garcia on alert. The 2nd AEG continued to be active at Diego Garcia until 21 April 1999, when it transferred to Fairford for Operation *Allied Force* (OAF).

The HQ building for the Director of Military Intelligence was one of a number of key command centres in Baghdad hit by CALCMs launched from B-52Hs during *Desert Fox*. These 'before and after' BDA photographs were shown in a Pentagon press briefing just hours after the weapons had hit their target, all but destroying it (*USAF*)

Although *Desert Fox* was a brief 'police action' lasting just four days, it introduced some new weapons to combat, including the B-1B Lancer, LANTIRN targeting pods for F-14 Tomcats and the AGM-130A air-to-ground missile. Coalition aircraft flew more than 656 combat sorties (all at night), hitting 97 military targets and firing 90 CALCMs, without suffering any losses. Thirteen targets allegedly associated with WMD production were hit, along with many others that were clearly intended to weaken Saddam Hussein's control of his military hegemony.

However, its long-term effects on the president were as unsuccessful as the attempted coup by the Iraqi Army's 3rd Corps at the same time. The dictator's sleeping quarters in Radwaniyah Palace in the outskirts of Baghdad was among the 49 first-night targets directly connected with his regime. A hit on the building that contained Saddam Hussein and his entourage would not have been lamented by those who planned and executed *Desert Fox*. Targeting did not include the bulk of Iraq's military assets or even some of the suspected WMD manufacturing sites, which were impossible to identify exactly.

The DoD assessed that the results for the 90 CALCM launches from B-52Hs were far more destructive than those during *Desert Strike*, when only 13 Block 0 examples with 2000-lb warheads were launched, or in *Desert Storm*, when 35 Block 0s were released by B-52Gs. In four days the majority of the selected targets had been destroyed or sufficiently degraded. This allowed Secretary of Defense William Cohen to claim that 'Saddam's missile program has been set back by at least a year'.

*Desert Fox* was the most determined use of Coalition offensive power in the period between *Desert Storm* and *Iraqi Freedom*, and it demonstrated that the US could launch large-scale attacks from carriers in the Northern Arabian Gulf and bombers from Diego Garcia without having to rely on any specific Gulf states for basing rights. As previously noted, US and British forces involved in the operation suffered no losses, and the higher proportion of PGMs delivered (compared with *Desert Storm*) achieved more accurate results overall. No SAM launches were reported by aircrew.

Inert ALCMs on their complex transporter are moved into position for loading into the bomb-bay of a 2nd BW B-52H at Barksdale AFB in August 2020. These 20 ft-long missiles are externally similar in appearance to the 90 CALCMs employed to such devastating effect in *Desert Fox* (*USAF/T Panopalis Archives*)

Civilian casualties were fewer, and there were more successes in targeting major leadership targets. Anti-aircraft opposition was ineffective, although this did not prevent Saddam Hussein from announcing an Iraqi victory.

Many assumed that regime change was actually the main, unspoken goal of *Desert Fox*, although the comment that came nearest to an official opinion on that subject was made by the Chairman of the Joint Chiefs of Staff, Gen Henry Shelton, when he stated that the end of Saddam Hussein's reign would be 'value added'.

By 23 December all six B-1Bs and 12 of the 15 B-52Hs at Diego Garcia had returned to the USA, but they remained on 72 hours' notice to return if needed. *Desert Fox* was followed by a steady increase in smaller-scale attacks on Iraq's military and, in particular, its leaders in the hope of weakening Saddam Hussein's grip on the nation. NFZs became areas in which offensive military action was permitted with the aim of initiating regime change, and one such event included an air strike on a military base near Mosul.

A steady build-up of air attacks to a regular total of one per three days from December 1998 to February 1999 progressively damaged Iraq's elaborate air defence systems, while an increasing number of SAM and AAA batteries were moved into southern Iraq. There were also more than 70 NFZ violations committed by IrAF aircraft, including 20 incidents where air-to-air missiles were fired – unsuccessfully – at US aircraft. In 1999 alone, 450 targets were struck by 1800 bombs.

By the late summer of 2002, Operation *Southern Watch*, the 11-year imposition of a NFZ south of the 33rd parallel, had evolved into *Southern Focus*, with attacks on Iraqi air defence sites to help prepare the way for B-52Hs and other bombers to reach their targets when OIF I commenced. The cable repeater stations which linked Iraq's command and control network were among the 391 targets hit during this period. The attacks were justified by Iraq's persistent attempts to shoot down Coalition aircraft flying the patrol missions for *Southern Focus*.

*Desert Fox* gave both US politicians and generals the confidence to employ similar limited, but carefully targeted, measures against the Federal Republic of Yugoslavia (FRY) in March–June 1999. To its critics, however, it was too limited and a mere show of strength that left Saddam Hussein securely in power with most of his military capability intact. However, its effect on the potential production of WMD was 'devastating' according to David Kay, leader of the Iraq Survey Group, causing the country's weapons programmes to lose all momentum and its technicians to become demoralised. The events of 11 September 2001 would considerably harden US policies regarding intransigent national leaders and potential sources of terrorism.

B-52Hs of the 96th EBS and KC-10As of the 305th Air Mobility Wing (AMW) share the ramp at Diego Garcia in December 1998 for Operation *Desert Fox*. Despite covering only 11.5 square miles of terrain, the British-owned island offers a 12,000 ft concrete runway that is perfect for heavy aircraft operations (*USAF/T Panopalis Archives*)

# CHAPTER TWO
# ALLIED FORCE

With heavy use beginning to abrade its paint finish, B-52H-160-BW 60-0059 *THE DEVIL'S OWN*, complete with 96th BS flagship markings, flew numerous Kosovo missions. Gunship Gray (FS 36118) B-52Hs began to emerge from the Air Logistics Centre in 1992, Program Depot Maintenance having seen the new scheme applied following an airframe 'strip and paint'. Fibreglass wingtips are covered to prevent them suffering stripping compound damage, and they are sometimes left unpainted. As seen here with 60-0059, they can appear white or, in this instance, a lighter shade of grey (*USAF*)

OAF was America's last military operation of the 20th century, the first in which NATO fought another nation as a military force and the last one in which aerial combat resulted in the destruction of aircraft. It was also the first time that all three US strategic bombers – B-52H, B-1B and B-2A – were involved in the same combat operation. At the time, half the USAF's assets were committed to this and other related operations, including around a quarter of its bombers and 44 per cent of its fighters, compared with only 15 per cent during *Desert Storm*. The heaviest demands were on the tanker force to enable B-52Hs and other aircraft to make the long flights to targets in the area. More than 80 per cent of USAF tanker crews were called to action, including AFRC forces.

The civil war which marked the break-up of the Socialist Federal Republic of Yugoslavia after 1990 began when President Slobodan Milošević took control of the nationalistic Serbian minority in Kosovo. Serb forces in Bosnia-Herzegovina declared independence and began forcibly expelling Muslims (who were covertly supported by the USA) and Croats from the country in a policy of ethnic cleansing. Open conflict continued from 1991 to 1995, culminating in NATO's Operation *Deliberate Force* from August 1995, when NATO allies became more effective at working together, while the USA took the dominant role.

The Serbian leadership's refusal to seek a settlement formally ended with the Dayton Peace Accord in December 1995 and the insertion of a 60,000-strong NATO-led peace Implementation Force into Bosnia-Herzegovina. Throughout this frustrating period, NATO and the UN found themselves in a bafflingly complex, divisive situation in which agreement between the allies was often elusive and the passive role of a peacekeeping force was tested to the limits. The UN also enforced a no-fly zone over Bosnia-Herzegovina from April 1993 in Operation *Deny Flight*.

Air activity extended to CAS (code-named *Blue Sword*) for the peacekeeping force in Bosnia-Herzegovina. It relied on tactical aircraft, often using the patrolling fighters from Italian bases carrying air-to-ground ordnance. However, a lack of PGMs made exact targeting with a minimum risk of collateral damage hard to attain. Locating the small, well-dispersed targets such as tanks and artillery was hard due to difficult terrain and consistently poor weather.

## OPERATION *DELIBERATE FORCE*

The list of potential targets for this operation, from 20 August to 30 September 1995, included radar and communications sites, factories and bridges. To minimise the possibility of collateral damage, PGMs were specified for most missions. As the target list expanded there were civilian casualties, and the world's press began to question the length of the campaign.

The absence of heavy bombers for *Deliberate Force* had practical and political origins. They were not needed to enforce *Deny Flight*, although 917th Wing B-52Hs did deploy to Aviano AB, Italy, in December 1993, August 1994 and May 1995 in a show of strength. The likelihood of collateral damage was another reason. Area bombing of larger targets like factories and ammunition dumps once the extensive Serb missile and AAA air defences had been suppressed, or launching ALCMs, was not required for this operation. However, both types of mission would be allocated to B-52Hs in later Balkans conflicts.

In 2000 Col Robert C Owen commented in the Air University's official final report on *Deliberate Force*, 'Even had a significant military reason existed to bring heavy bombers into the fight, *Deliberate Force* commanders likely would have had second thoughts, given the big airplane's inherent political liability of signalling escalation'. To Maj Gen Hal Hornberg, directing the Combined Air Operations Centre (CAOC) at Vicenza, in Italy, 'Employing heavy bombers would have meant "going beyond the psychological threshold" of the campaign and could have had an adverse effect on the Bosnian Serb peace process'. Sadly, President Milošević was obviously unmoved by the possibility of an attack by America's 'big stick'.

In any case, as Col Owen observed, 'the shorter-range strike aircraft already available in-theatre were capable of "servicing" all planned targets within all the available constraints of time and precision. This was also true of the Stratofortress's precision strike capabilities. Whatever the B-52H's CALCMs could do in terms of performing precision strikes and minimising risks from the Serbian air defences, other aircraft weapons systems combinations and the US Navy's [ship-launched] Tomahawk missiles could also do'. PGMs were specified for all strikes after 30 August 1995.

By 14 September almost all the Phase One and Two targets had been destroyed, and UN/NATO leaders were reluctant to proceed with hitting Phase Three's 'big' targets even though the Serb leaders had not backed down. Faced with a successful Croatian and Bosnian Muslim counter-offensive on the ground, as well as a more determined UN/NATO air campaign, President Milošević finally agreed on 14 September to cease hostilities and withdraw the siege of Sarajevo. However, an offensive on the crucial western Serb city of Banja Luka by Bosnian and Croat forces continued.

## OPERATION *ALLIED FORCE*

Fighting between Serb forces and the Kosovo Liberation Army (KLA) began again early in 1998, and the situation quickly deteriorated despite UN Security Council resolutions and energetic international diplomacy. Serb police drove 230,000 ethnic Albanians from their Kosovo homes while NATO prepared air strikes. On 12 October 1998, President Milošević, who refused to negotiate with Albanian leaders or surrender any territory, was told that air strikes would begin unless his ethnic cleansing activities ceased. This ultimatum was backed by the deployment of US air assets, including B-52Hs to Europe.

In Exercise *Determined Falcon* in mid-June 1998, 98 NATO aircraft had operated from Italian bases, flying over Macedonia and Albania up to the borders of Kosovo. Aviano continued to provide the focus for these initiatives, as it had done for Operations *Decisive Edge* in 1996 and *Deliberate Guard* from 1997, both of which monitored Serb activity in the areas of potential conflict.

A limited air campaign was ordered on 13 October 1998. Seven B-52Hs from Barksdale were deployed to the 16th Air Expeditionary Wing (AEW) at Fairford, among other NATO air assets throughout Europe. Launched from Barksdale at 2000 hrs on 10 October, they began to arrive at Fairford at midday on the 11th. These aircraft joined KC-135s, RC-135s and F-15Cs within the 16th AEW.

President Milošević responded to this deterrent gesture by pausing his aggression in line with the Dayton Peace Accords, allowing the 2nd BW contingent to return to Louisiana. NATO reconnaissance in Operation *Eagle Eye* from 29 October 1998 saw USAF U-2s and MQ-1 Predators overflying Kosovo to verify the removal of Serbian forces. However, by February 1999 FRY incursions and genocide had resumed, and a limited air campaign was planned to force the Serbs to negotiate a full settlement.

*"The Mad Bolshevik"* (B-52H-140-BW 60-0020) awaits its next OAF mission, the aircraft being armed with eight GBU-10s. These PGMs were transported to Fairford, but not by B-52s. Stratofortresses flying from the Gloucestershire air base during the 1990s used ordnance sourced from the largest USAFE bomb dump in Europe, sited at nearby RAF Welford, Berkshire. Three B-52Hs could deliver as much conventional ordnance in one mission as a US Navy carrier air wing could drop per day. Aside from expending LGBs, *"The Mad Bolshevik"*, flagship of the 20th BS/2nd BW, launched ten CALCMs during the course of 17 OAF missions. Deployed several times during the operation, it was among 17 B-52Hs rotated in as replacements. Retired to storage at AMARG in 2008, it has been maintained ever since as a potential replacement airframe (*Author*)

Phase One of the campaign was intended to degrade President Milošević's considerable Soviet-supplied air defences. A second phase would attack military facilities and troop concentrations below the 44th parallel, before extending the target list to other areas of Yugoslavia with the optimistic aim of forcing the Serbs to finally back down. As a Pentagon spokesman commented, 'We miscalculated. We thought that when the bombing started Milošević would play the victim, not turn into Adolf Hitler Jr'.

NATO authorised its second large-scale combat operation, exclusively an air campaign, on 22 March 1999, and it occurred between 24 March and 10 June. All three of the USAF's heavy bomber types were used for OAF (known in the USA as Operation *Noble Anvil*) – the defence of secessionist Kosovar Albanians in Kosovo from suppression by the forces of the FRY, consisting of Serbia and Montenegro. Prompted by the ethnic cleansing of Albanians by FRY forces, who killed more than 8700 Kosovar Albanian civilians and drove 848,000 into exile from Kosovo, NATO reacted on humanitarian grounds without the approval of China and Russia in the UN Security Council.

NATO reinforced its air elements in anticipation of further strikes in the Balkans, while President Clinton remained adamant that American troops would not be 'put in Kosovo to fight a war'. More than 250 aircraft (200 of them American) were soon assembled at European bases, organised from the CAOC at Da Molin AB, Vicenza, which developed daily air tasking orders.

This time B-52Hs were the first reinforcements to arrive, with seven B-52Hs from the 2nd and one from the 5th BWs being deployed to Fairford on 21–22 February as the basis of the 2nd Expeditionary Operations Group. The 20th BS was appointed lead unit for the operation, but aircraft and crews also came from the 11th BS.

As in *Desert Fox*, the B-52Hs would initiate the operation, and they flew their first practice sorties on 9 March. Air refuelling was provided by the KC-135Rs of the 366th Wing's 22nd Air Refueling Squadron (ARS) from Mountain Home AFB, Idaho. Additional KC-135R and KC-10A tankers were sent to RAF Mildenhall, Sicily and Spain. Aircraft from the 55th ARS and the Alabama and Wisconsin Air National Guard (ANG) supplemented Mildenhall's 100th Expeditionary ARW, deploying to RAF Brize Norton, in Oxfordshire, to feed the growing fleet of USAF bombers.

The B-52H crews were drawn from the 2nd and 5th BWs. Two more Minot B-52Hs arrived at Fairford on 29 April, although only three from the 5th BW appeared there in total. Additional bombers from the 23rd BS at Minot and from Barksdale, with 'Tiger' callsigns, landed at Fairford on 1 May. One aircraft (60-0016) was used as the crew trainer and local familiarisation 'bounce bird', as well as for numerous CALCM missions. Several crews had flown conventional bombing missions during *Desert Fox*, although very few

B-52H crews from both the 2nd and 5th BWs are briefed on their targets in the FRY at Fairford during the early stages of OAF. While in England, their operations were overseen by the 2nd AEG. Personnel assigned to fly the mission have removed unit insignia and name tags from their flight suits (*USAF*)

A USAF armourer transports an AGM-86C CALCM across a damp Fairford flightline towards waiting B-52H-155-BW 60-0051 *APPETITE FOR DESTRUCTION II* of the 23rd BS on 30 March 1999. This aircraft was one of five Stratofortresses sent from Minot to Fairford for OAF (*USAF*)

had *Desert Storm* experience. Unlike the hard-pressed tanker crews, they usually got a day off between missions, but like the B-1Bs, the B-52Hs, commanded by Col Floyd Carpenter, averaged two to four sorties daily.

After two seven-aircraft mass launch practice missions, the Fairford B-52Hs went into action on the night of 24 March following a route called the Atlantic Loop, taking them south from Britain and across the Mediterranean. Apart from attacks in Kosovo after 26 March, almost all missions were flown at night.

The initial strikes were made by eight Fairford-based 20th EBS B-52Hs, taking off at 1042 hrs local time as 'Havoc 11–18', including two which turned back – an unarmed decoy and an air spare. Inflight refuelling was provided over the Atlantic by Mildenhall-based KC-135Rs. After 31 March, five KC-135Rs from the 366th, with 'Riyal' callsigns, deployed to Fairford for refuelling duties. They duly supported more than 600 aircraft during the operation. The B-52Hs were filmed on lift-off by CNN television cameras, thereby warning the FRY's air defences of the threat and reinforcing the 'show of force' concept worldwide. Sadly, even as the B-52Hs approached their targets late in the evening, the Belgrade military leaders still considered themselves immune to attack from NATO aircraft.

The Stratofortresses each carried eight AGM-86C CALCMs internally for delivery against the FRY air defence system's command hubs at a distance, rather than overflying targets. This tactic was not anticipated by the Serbian leadership, who assumed that, as in *Deliberate Force*, CALCMs would only be used against the more difficult, inaccessible or well-defended targets that could not be eliminated by conventional bombing. 'Havoc 12' from the 20th EBS fired the first missile, replacing 'Havoc 11' in that position after it experienced problems with two missiles. 'Havoc 12's' crew were able to make some rapid updates to their CALCMs' data and managed to launch five of their eight missiles on schedule.

The CALCMs, fitted with blast fragmentation warheads, had GPS guidance towards 'soft' targets, and they were fired at one-minute intervals. The aircraft also used the recent installation of the Multi-Source Task System, which provided updates on weather, targets and threat warnings, managed by personnel from Air Force Space Command at Schriever AFB, Colorado. CALCM launches coincided with a volley of TLAMs from US Navy warships. Additional air strikes on airfields in Serbia and Kosovo contributed to the first night's total of 400 sorties against 40 targets.

The B-52s' mission included a 13-hour trip southwards, around Spain, over the Mediterranean (crossing Malta) and into a specially-reserved corridor across central Italy to reduce mission time before reaching their CALCM launch point. As they approached the Balkans, but still hundreds of miles from their targets, the bombers moved into strike formation and received final targeting information from an orbiting E-3 Airborne Warning and Control System (AWACS) and other relevant information from an RC-135 *Rivet Joint* reconnaissance aircraft. The route was partly an echo of the southern *Chrome Dome* route that nuclear-armed B-52s flew during the Cold War.

CALCMs were then launched at one-minute intervals, with two or three missiles programmed for each target. Once fired, the CALCMs could not be 'contacted' electronically, re-routed or self-destructed. Deconfliction with missiles from other aircraft and submarines was obviously a top priority.

Mk 84 GP bombs with nose plugs for impact fusing fill the MAU-12/A racks of a 20th BS B-52H at Fairford in May 1999. 'CP' ('common pylon') stencilled codes often appeared on Barksdale's bomb racks at this time (*USAF/T Panopalis Archives*)

One MiG-29 from the Air Force of Serbia and Montenegro was launched to intercept the B-52Hs, but its radar warning system failed and the aircraft was shot down, as was a second one, by escorting NATO fighters. Two others had to return to base with inoperative weapons systems or combat damage. Following these losses, the remaining FRY fighter units were told to remain on the ground. B-1B 85-0083 was subsequently adorned with four MiG-21 and seven helicopter 'kill' markings on its nose-gear door, the crew having claimed these as destroyed on the ground.

Targets near Pristina, capital city of Kosovo (whose residents had been warned of the imminent B-52 bombing via a graphic leaflet drop), and Batajnica air base were hit on 24–25 March. Strikes on a power generating plant cut off electricity to the capital, while subsequent attacks targeted SAM sites and 23 air defence radars and control centres, with each B-52 releasing missiles at up to three objectives. Degrading the air defences allowed the numerous tactical strike aircraft to hit pinpoint targets with PGMs.

Seventy-eight CALCMS were launched by B-52Hs in the early stages of the conflict, with 61-0016 on record as firing the most with 15 missiles, followed by 61-0023 with 11 launches in 16 missions and 60-0020 with ten in 17 missions. 61-0016's high score was partly because it was the last CALCM-configured B-52H still at Fairford after progressive rotation of the others. One crew experienced a CALCM separating from its launcher but not leaving the bomb-bay. That B-52 had to return to Fairford with a 'hung' cruise missile resting against its bomb-bay doors, posing a problem for its armament crew. Other CALCMs from the 30 fired during the first week of OAF were seen to fail, including no fewer than six during the third night of the operation (although some of them were not physically launched, as their systems did not show 100 per cent readiness).

The rapid depletion of CALCM stocks resulted in some B-52Hs having to launch with partial loads from 1 May. Only 238 CALCMs were in the inventory in December 1998, and after the opening attacks against Kosovo, that number had dropped to 70 missiles. Three aircraft flew directly from Diego Garcia with missiles to boost the stocks, but the remaining CALCMs were reserved for the decreasing number of high-value targets or for limited use in the frequent periods of bad weather. Conventional ordnance in the form of 500-lb Mk 82 and 2000-lb Mk 84 General Purpose (GP) bombs became more commonly used, as they had been in *Desert Storm*. B-52Hs could carry 45 of the former internally and on HSABs and 18 of the latter, usually in combination with Mk 82s.

Aside from the CALCMs employed by the B-52Hs, missiles were also launched from US Navy ships and a Royal Navy submarine in the Mediterranean. These weapons damaged a number of radar sites and aircraft shelters. Although more than 120 SA-3 missiles were also destroyed when their storage facility was struck, the FRY's air defences generally remained operational. However, degrading the country's military infrastructure through high-altitude attacks reduced the risks posed to NATO aircraft from the FRY's well-equipped air defence system.

In mid-1995, the Bosnian Serb Army's SAM air defence units numbered seven ex-Soviet batteries with SA-2F Mod 5 'Guidelines' and 16 batteries operating SA-6 'Gainful' (9M9 Kub). It also had more than 1000 AAA pieces, which, along with the SAMs, were all managed by eight early warning radar sites. There were also many SA-7 'Grail' and SA-14 'Gremlin' man-portable air defence systems (MANPADS) in service with frontline troops, as well as SA-9 'Gaskin' and SA-13 'Gopher' infra-red seeking SAMs on vehicular mounts. Around 700 SAMs were fired at Allied aircraft during the campaign – three times as many as had been expended by the Iraqis in *Desert Storm*. All MANPADS and AAA posed a threat to aircraft at altitudes below 15,000 ft, while heavy bombers were at risk from the longer-range SA-2Fs and SA-6s.

Despite these significant threats, missions by two or three B-52Hs continued to be flown during the early stages of OAF – a four-ship take-off also occurred at 1330 hrs GMT on 26 March. Stratofortresses typically flew seven-hour *Combat Round Robin* missions to Kosovo, after which several jets returned directly to the USA to collect CALCMs. They would then fly back to Fairford with the missiles carried internally, as they could not be airlifted to England in transport aircraft. This requirement led to a rotational system involving 25 bombers cycling through Fairford.

Some CALCMs were airlifted to the airfield from Minot by five 23rd BS/5th BW B-52Hs, which arrived at Fairford on 27 March and then flew missions from there, and, as previously mentioned, by three Barksdale

*Eagle's Wrath III* (B-52H-165-BW 61-0002) flew to Fairford with ten GBU-10 LGBs onboard as a replacement aircraft during OAF. The Stratofortress is seen here, marked up as the 2nd OG flagship, during a 2020 flight from Eielson AFB, Alaska (*USAF*)

aircraft that had been on an alert detachment at Diego Garcia. The missiles were ferried internally, as carriage on the wing pylons, while boosting the number by 12, would have created extra drag, thereby increasing the need for aerial refuelling.

Of the 78 AGM-86Cs launched from B-52Hs early on, some 55 were expended on 24 March. There were several missile failures on each mission, so the use of multiple weapons proved to be essential, although it soon exhausted the supply of AGM-86Cs.

Prompted by the low stock of CALCMs, which had to be converted from nuclear-armed AGM-86Bs by the replacement of the nuclear warhead with 1000 lbs of conventional explosive, two aircraft (60-0020 and 61-0002) flew in to Fairford with ten 2000-lb GBU-10 LGBs on their pylons, although these were not delivered in combat. Two more (60-0062 and 60-0049, not among the four *Rapid Eight* aircraft initially modified to carry the AGM-142) arrived at Fairford in mid-May carrying AGM-142A Raptor Have Nap missiles based on the Rafael Popeye. Two were fired during OAF, with disappointing results, from these aircraft, which both had the AN/ASW-55 data link pod. B-52H 60-0049 was later seen with a mission 'score' marking for an AGM-142 alongside its five CALCM silhouettes and three conventional bomb markings.

Two Fairford-based B-52Hs kept up the pressure on the night of 27 March, and four additional aircraft were scheduled to be deployed to the base together with five B-1Bs. Three 5th BW B-52Hs arrived two days later. The maximum number of Stratofortresses at Fairford during OAF was 14 simultaneously, although 19 were deployed in total, including four which were rotated back to the USA and six sent as replacements or extras. Five of the 19 were from Minot AFB and the rest from the 11th, 20th and 96th BSs at Barksdale.

After the high-priority targets had been taken out, the CALCM-delivering B-52Hs became less vital and some were rotated in favour of those with conventional weapons capability. With a reduced air defence threat, the bombers also began to fly both day and night missions against area targets such as airfields and army compounds, dropping 45 Mk 82 (27 internally and 18 on the pylons) or 18 Mk 84 unguided bombs from around 40,000 ft. SUU-30/A CBUs were a frequent alternative load.

B-52H-160-BW 60-0062 *CAJUN FEAR* of the 20th BS/2nd BW was one of a pair of Stratofortresses that arrived at a rain-soaked Fairford in mid-May 1999 armed with AGM-142 Have Nap missiles. In OAF, B-52Hs were CALCM launchers early in the conflict and 'area bombers' later (*T Panopalis Archives*)

Gen Henry Shelton, Chairman of the Joint Chiefs of Staff, described 'three formidable challenges in the area. First was the integrated air defence system, second was the terrain and third was the weather'. Persistently poor weather over the battlefield, with at least 50 per cent cloud cover for much of the period, placed severe limitations on the use of LGBs, while the B-2As' JDAM could still achieve successes in those conditions. Their brief introduction was intended to supplement dwindling stocks of CALCMs, but operational results did not justify the continued use of these costly weapons.

Although the NATO target list ran to 976 sites at the start of OAF, some were vetoed by France for its own political reasons and others required extensive discussion with NATO partners. Despite most of the high-value targets being destroyed in the first three days of OAF, to the surprise of Allied leaders, there was no sign of capitulation by President Milošević, who firmly believed that the Serbs owned Kosovo. In fact, it would take three months of air operations to achieve NATO's aim.

## LANCERS, 'BUFFS' AND SPIRITS

Of the trio of USAF 'heavies' involved – the B-2A Spirit, B-52H Stratofortress and B-1B Lancer – the latter was the most heavily utilised, flying every day throughout the conflict for a total of 74 combat missions. Nine B-1Bs of the 28th BW's 34th, 37th and 77th BSs, based at Ellsworth AFB, and two from the 13th BS/7th BW at Dyess AFB were eventually deployed to Fairford on rotation with the 77th EBS/2nd AEG, joining B-52Hs managed by the 20th EBS and commanded by 96th BS CO Lt Col Timothy Leaptrott. The first five B-1Bs arrived on 1 April with 'Razor' callsigns. Rotation of the aircraft maintained six aircraft at Fairford at any time. A single B-2A (82-1067) visited Fairford on 10 March just to test the feasibility of using it as a base for the stealth bomber.

The USAF's bomber force in England was commanded by *Desert Strike* veteran Col Floyd L Carpenter.

Mixed strike packages would include two B-1Bs with Mk 82 bombs, two B-52Hs also with Mk 82s and KC-135R tankers from the 22nd Expeditionary Air Refueling Squadron, plus SEAD aircraft. Typical B-52H bombloads were nine Mk 82 bombs with BSU-33B/B conical fins on each Common Pylon Project wing HSAB and 27 more internally. Until the 1990s, Multiple Ejector Racks holding 12 Mk 82s each were available. From 3 April, the B-1Bs that deployed to Fairford from the USA alongside B-52Hs brought CALCMs with them.

Unlike the B-1B and B-52H, the B-2A could undertake a bombing mission without packages of SEAD and other support aircraft, aside from tankers and the jamming provided by US Marine Corps EA-6B Prowlers, which benefitted all the strike packages. The EA-6Bs were in fact so overworked that Gen Wesley Clark, Supreme Allied Commander Europe, issued an urgent request for additional aircraft to compensate for the USAF's recently retired EF-111A Raven jammers. The B-52 Systems Program Office at Tinker AFB, Oklahoma, instigated an urgent design initiative to fit AN/ALQ-99 ECM pods to the B-52H, making it an EB-52H. Modification of one aircraft was underway when the Kosovo campaign ended, and the role was eventually performed by the EA-18G Growler instead.

Complete with a targeting pod beneath its right wing, B-52H-155-BW 60-0049 – one of the two AGM-142 'porters' to Fairford in May 1999 – makes a smoky cartridge start. In the B-52H, Pratt and Whitney TF33-P-3 turbofans replaced the long-serving J57s of previous models, removing the requirement for water injection to boost the engines on take-off. In 1974, Project *Quick Start* added a cartridge start facility to each TF33 for a simultaneous start so as to minimise the reaction time for Cold War alert aircraft (*USAF*)

FRY air defences were managed more skilfully than similar installations encountered in the Gulf War and Operation *Deliberate Force*, making them more problematic for B-52Hs and other bombers when it came to overflying targets, rather than using stand-off weapons. Both previous US operations had been carefully studied by Yugoslav defence technicians, which meant that the SEAD effort became more complex and demanding.

US aircraft launched AGM-141 Tactical Air-Launched Decoys to make the Serb radar operators 'come up', followed by AGM-88 High-Speed Anti-Radiation Missiles (HARM). A typical response from FRY operators during *Deliberate Force* came on 7 September 1995, when they waited until HARM had been fired before switching off the SAM tracking radars, including some ex-US Army Westinghouse AN/TPS-70 sets. On that occasion, 33 HARM were fired, but only one SAM battery was damaged.

During OAF, SAM avoidance by creating no-fly areas around known SAM sites tended to replace SAM suppression in order to minimise risk. This soon severely limited air activity over Bosnia-Herzegovina. Skilful enemy tactics, dispersal of air defence assets and the generally poor weather slowed the NATO effort to the point where the number of targets hit in the first 12 hours of *Desert Storm* took 12 days to equal in the Kosovo campaign.

In early May, with the conflict dragging on, the 20th EBS began flying conventional bombing missions with 45 Mk 82 or M117 bombs or 18 Mk 84s. The B-52H CEM included provision of the HSAB in place of the previous I-beam adapter, and the former could each take nine Mk 82s, M117s or CBUs. Mk 84s, GBU-10/12 Paveway IIs, Mk 40 mines and AGM-84E Stand-off Land Attack Missiles could also be attached, as well as AGM-142A Have Nap for several aircraft and AGM-84E Harpoon for four others. SEAD support was invariably provided. US Secretary of Defence William Cohen announced the deployment of eight more 2nd BW B-52Hs and two from the 5th BW to Fairford on 27 April, five of them able to launch Have Nap.

After the FRY's air defences had been sufficiently degraded, the available targets in Serbia mainly required area bombing rather than the PGMs used by B-2As and later tactical fighter packages. As B-52Hs rotated through Fairford, an increasing number carried HSABs for iron bombs rather than CALCMs, thus allowing them to *(text continues on page 46)*

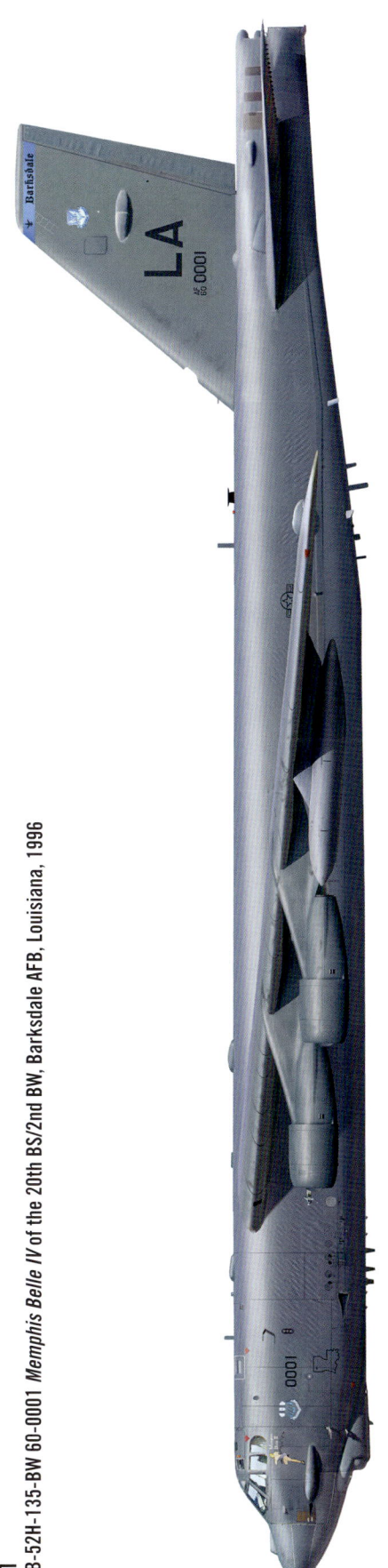

**1**
B-52H-135-BW 60-0001 *Memphis Belle IV* of the 20th BS/2nd BW, Barksdale AFB, Louisiana, 1996

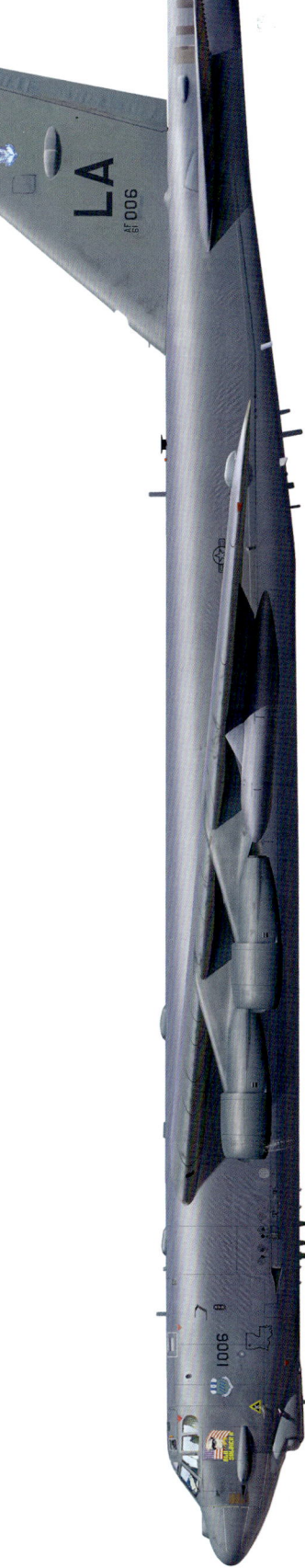

**2**
B-52H-165-BW 61-0006 *OLD SOLDIER II* of the 11th BS/2nd BW, Diego Garcia, December 1998

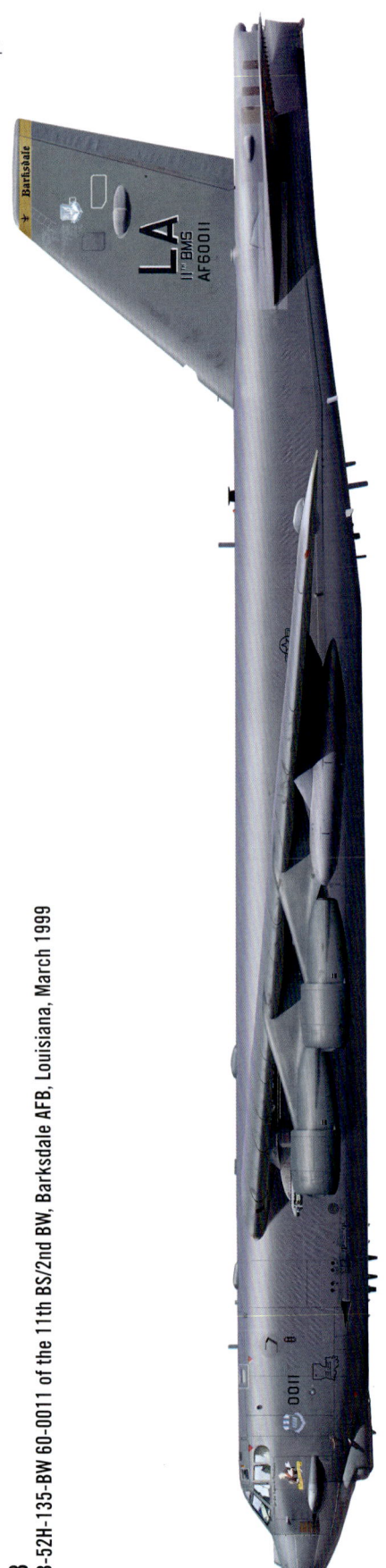

**3**
B-52H-135-BW 60-0011 of the 11th BS/2nd BW, Barksdale AFB, Louisiana, March 1999

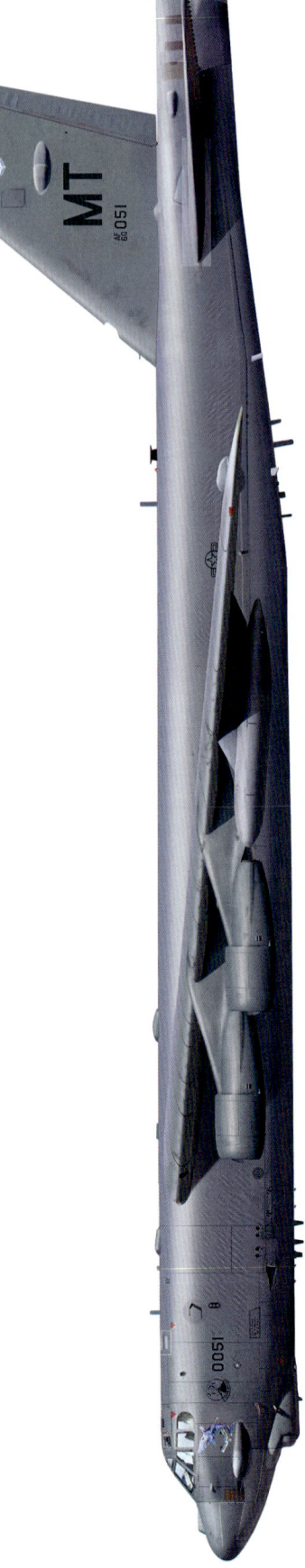

**4**
B-52H-155-BW 60-0051 *APPETITE FOR DESTRUCTION II* of the 23rd BS/5th BW, RAF Fairford, Gloucestershire, March 1999

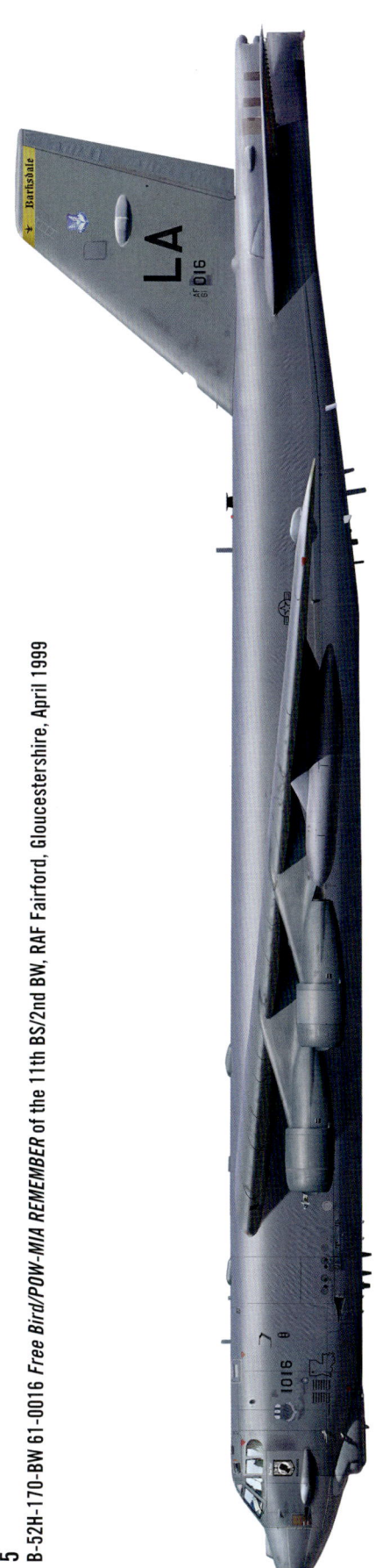

**5**
B-52H-170-BW 61-0016 *Free Bird/POW-MIA REMEMBER* of the 11th BS/2nd BW, RAF Fairford, Gloucestershire, April 1999

**6**
B-52H-160-BW 60-0062 *CAJUN FEAR* of the 20th BS/2nd BW, RAF Fairford, Gloucestershire, April 1999

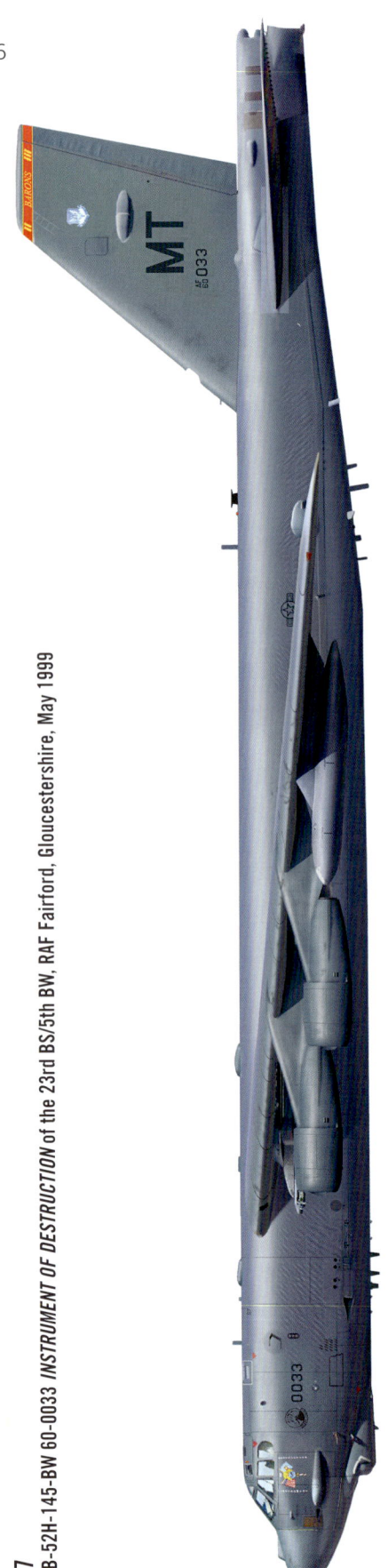

**7**
B-52H-145-BW 60-0033 *INSTRUMENT OF DESTRUCTION* of the 23rd BS/5th BW, RAF Fairford, Gloucestershire, May 1999

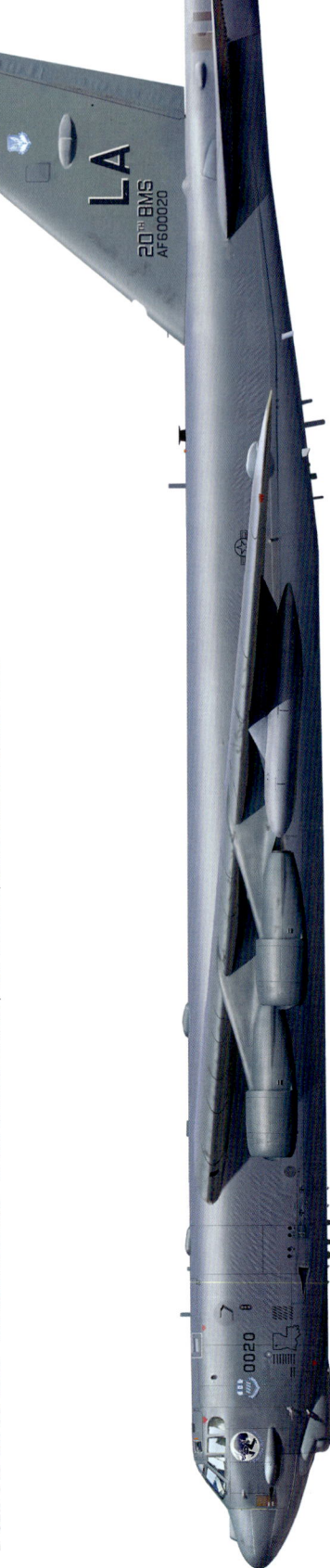

**8**
B-52H-140-BW 60-0020 *"The Mad Bolshevik"* of the 20th BS/2nd BW, RAF Fairford, Gloucestershire, June 1999

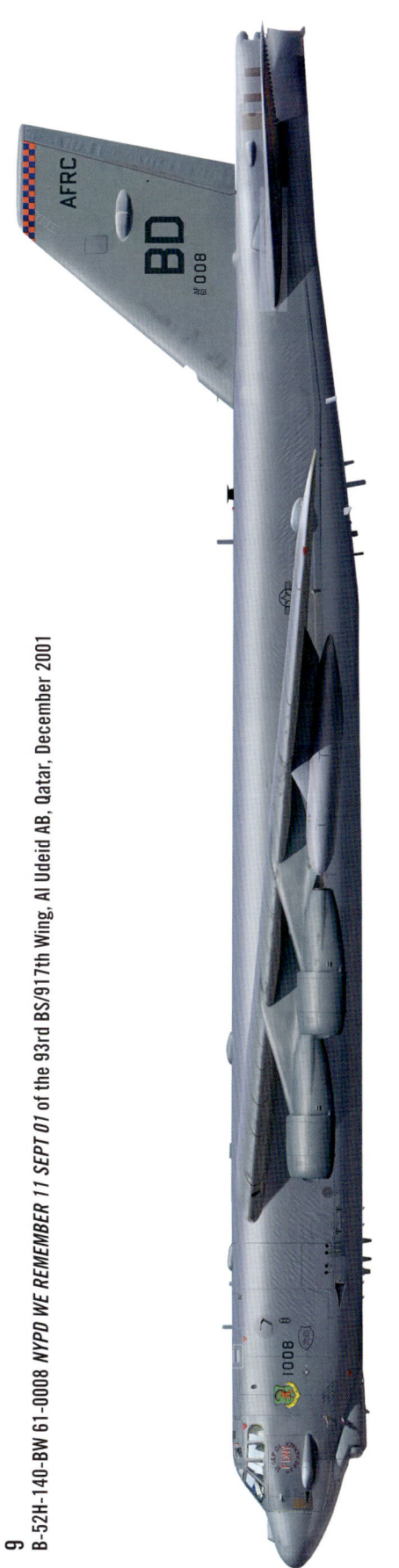

**9**
B-52H-140-BW 61-0008 *NYPD WE REMEMBER 11 SEPT 01* of the 93rd BS/917th Wing, Al Udeid AB, Qatar, December 2001

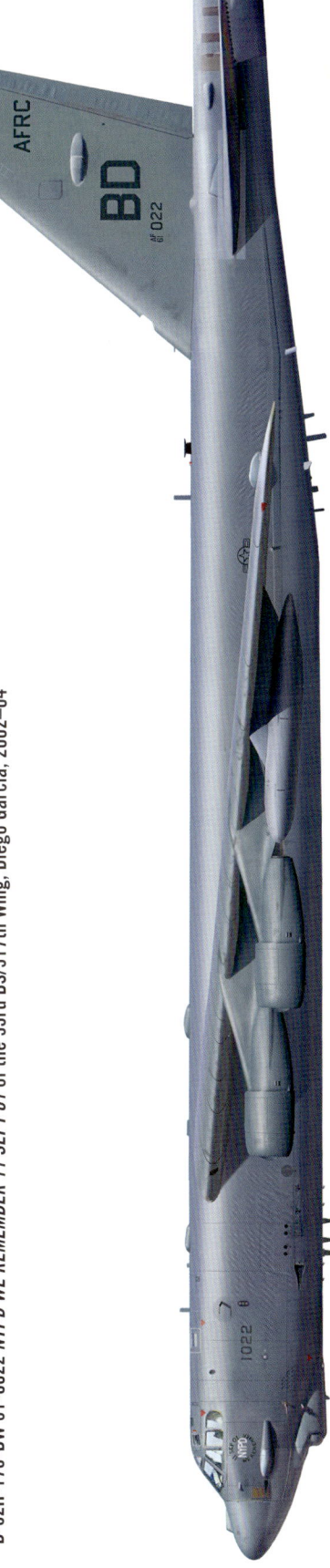

**10**
B-52H-170-BW 61-0022 *NYPD WE REMEMBER 11 SEPT 01* of the 93rd BS/917th Wing, Diego Garcia, 2002–04

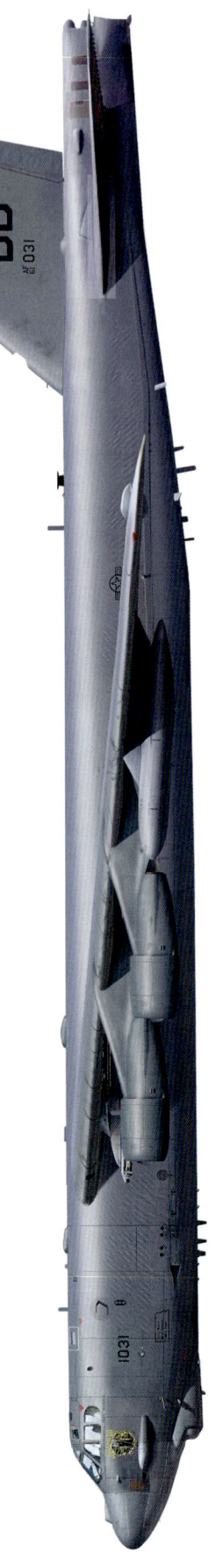

**11**
B-52H-175-BW 61-0029 *SAC TIME* of the 93rd BS/917th Wing, Barksdale AFB, Louisiana, 2004

**12**
B-52H-175-BW 61-0031 *JUDGMENT DAY* of the 93rd BS/917th Wing, Barksdale AFB, Louisiana, December 2014

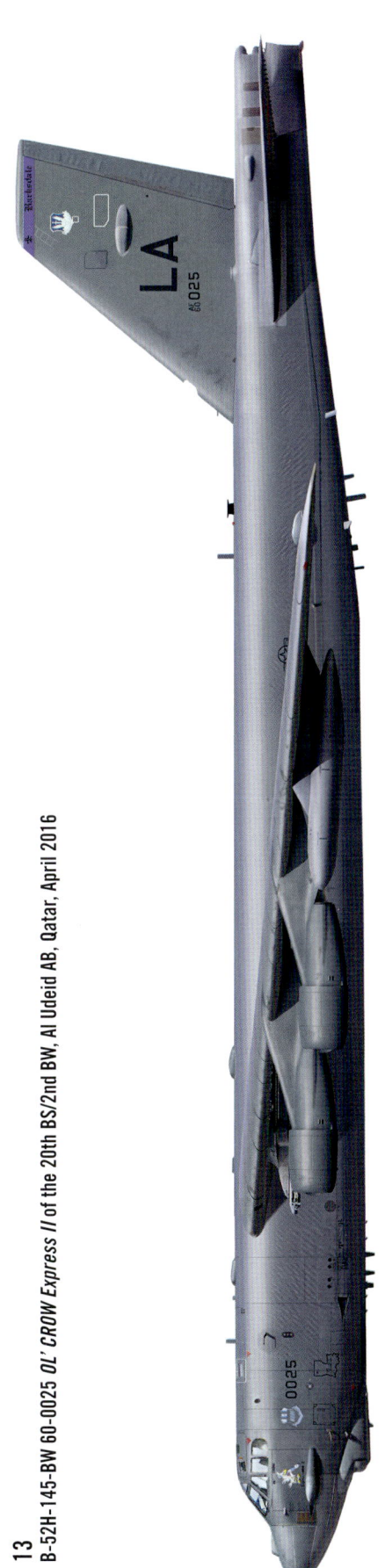

**13**
B-52H-145-BW 60-0025 *OL' CROW Express II* of the 20th BS/2nd BW, Al Udeid AB, Qatar, April 2016

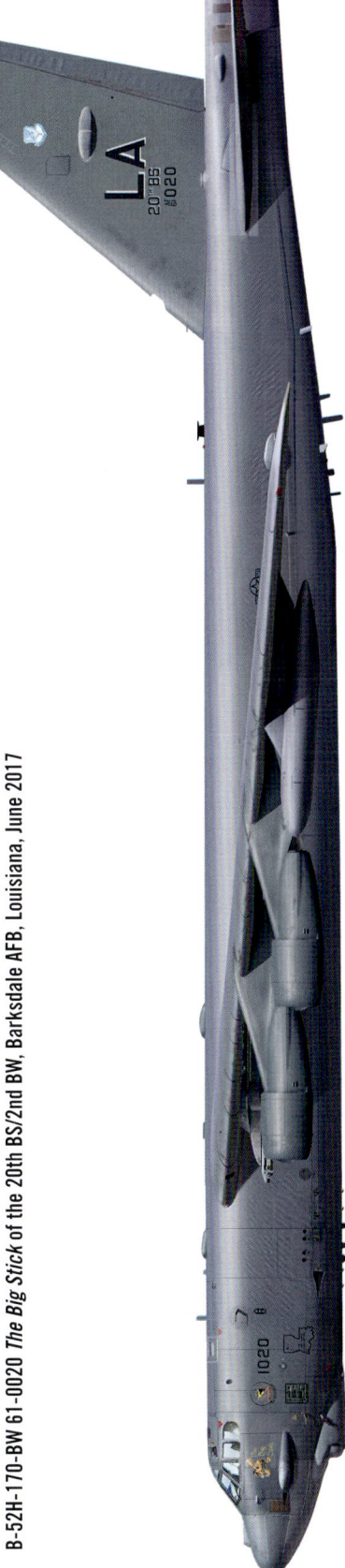

**14**
B-52H-170-BW 61-0020 *The Big Stick* of the 20th BS/2nd BW, Barksdale AFB, Louisiana, June 2017

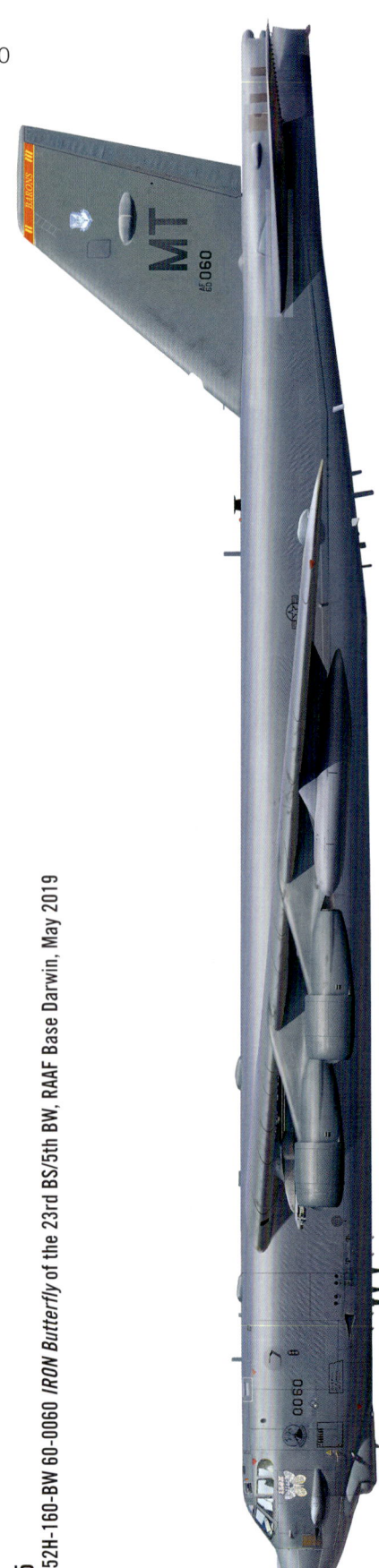

**15**
B-52H-160-BW 60-0060 *IRON Butterfly* of the 23rd BS/5th BW, RAAF Base Darwin, May 2019

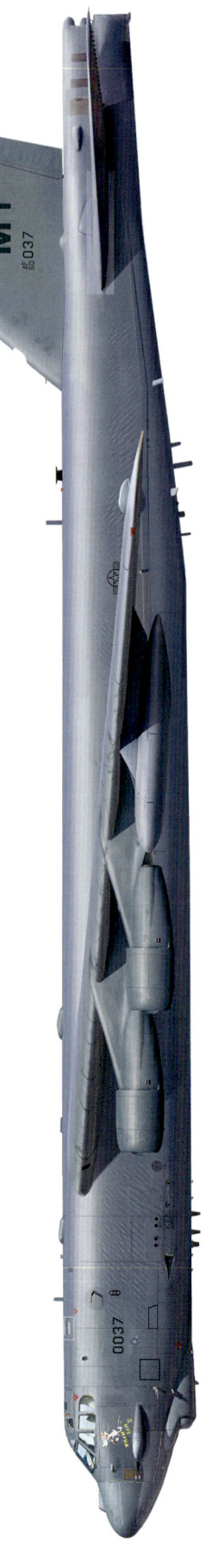

**16**
B-52H-150-BW 60-0037 *WHAM BAM II* of the 69th EBS/5th BW, Andersen AFB, Guam, July 2019

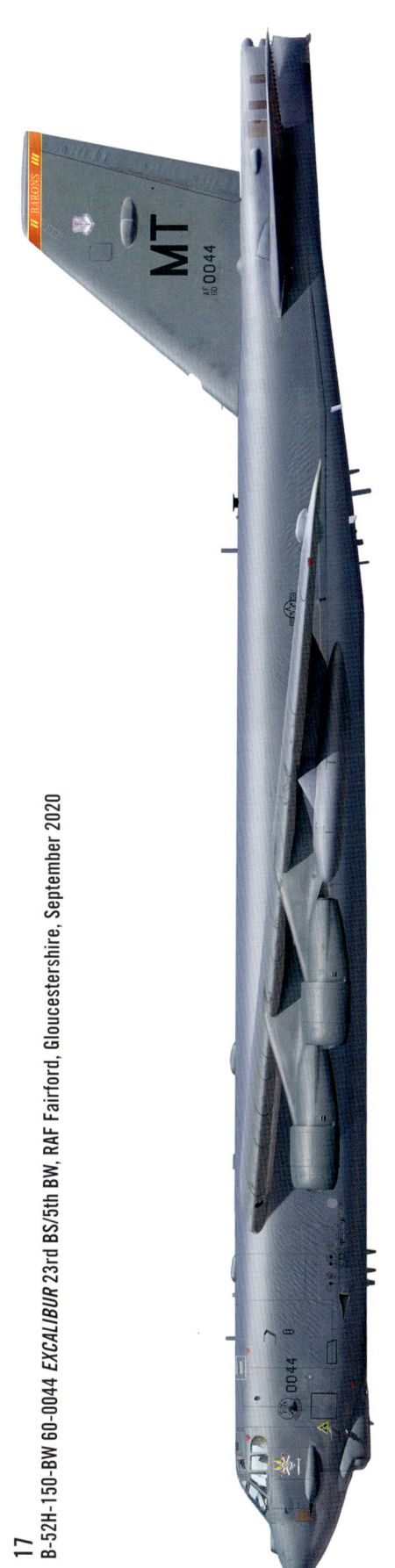

**17**
B-52H-150-BW 60-0044 *EXCALIBUR* 23rd BS/5th BW, RAF Fairford, Gloucestershire, September 2020

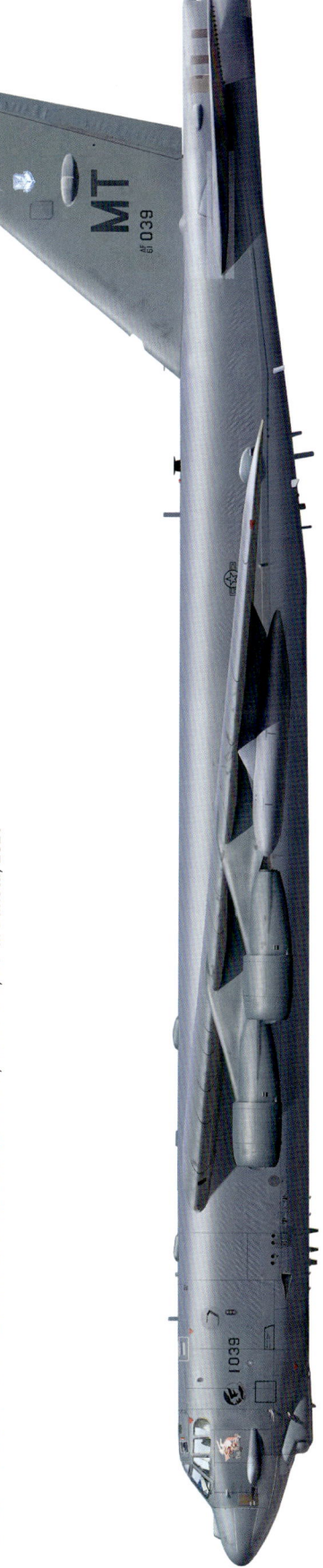

**18**
B-52H-175-BW 61-0039 *THE WARRIOR* of the 69th BS/5th BW, Minot AFB, North Dakota, 2021

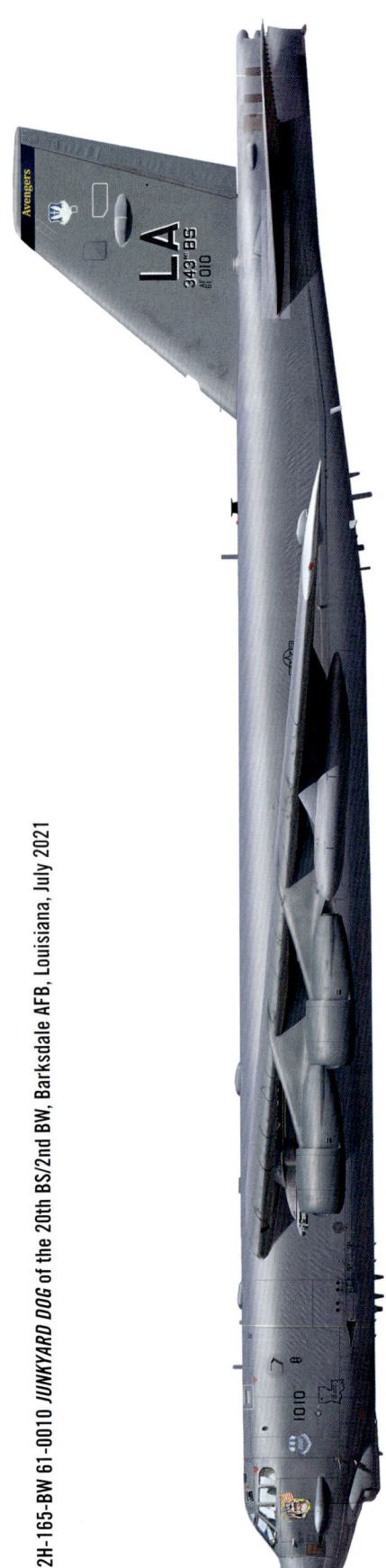

**19**
B-52H-165-BW 61-0010 *JUNKYARD DOG* of the 20th BS/2nd BW, Barksdale AFB, Louisiana, July 2021

**20**
B-52H-160-BW 60-0059 *THE DEVIL'S OWN* of the 96th BS/2nd BW, Barksdale AFB, Louisiana, 2022

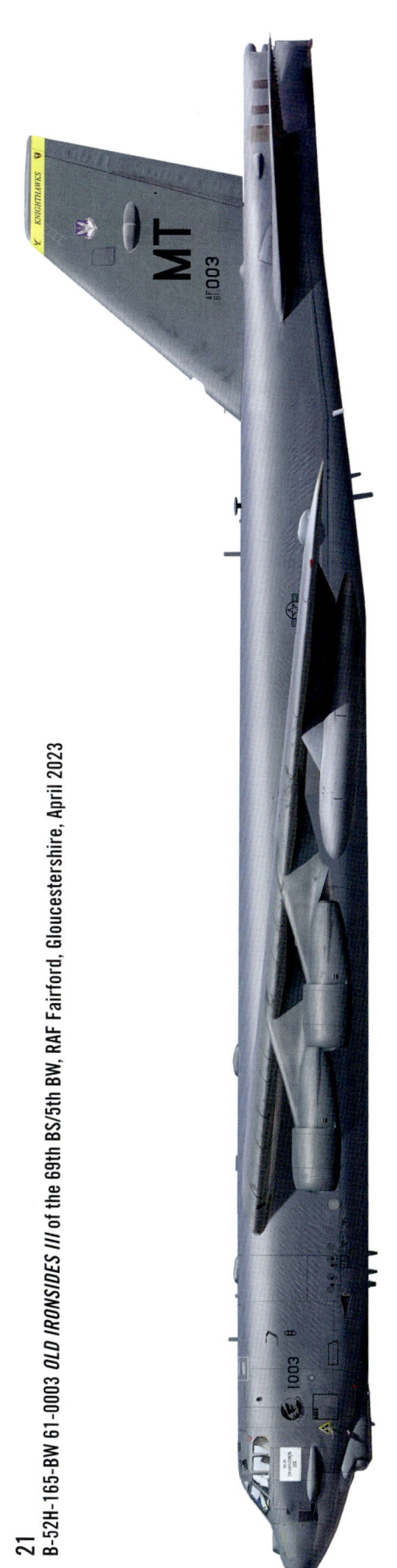

**21**
B-52H-165-BW 61-0003 *OLD IRONSIDES III* of the 69th BS/5th BW, RAF Fairford, Gloucestershire, April 2023

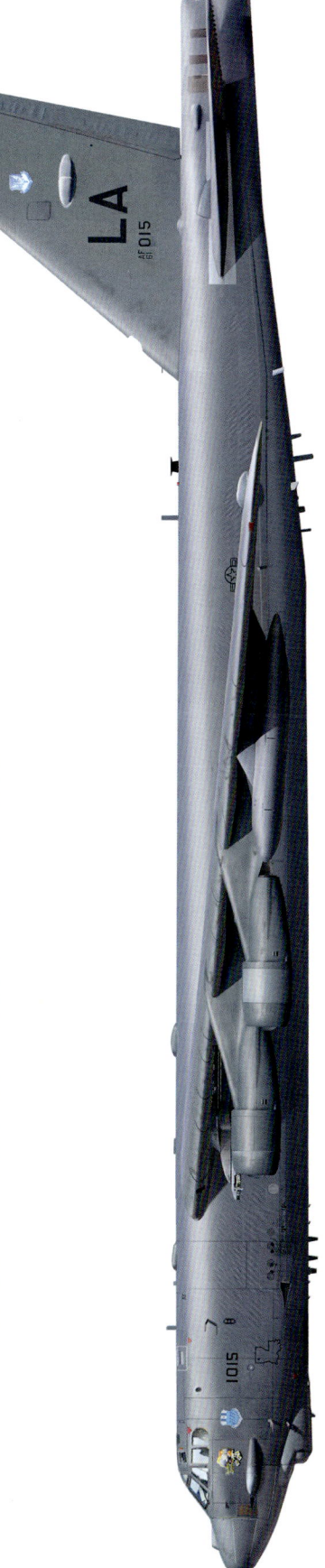

**22**
B-52H-170-BW 61-0015 *The Last Laugh* of the 96th EBS/2nd BW, Andersen AFB, Guam, March–July 2023

execute the first 'carpet bombing' missions undertaken in Europe since World War 2. The initial attacks, on 4 May, were against the Serb 243rd Motorised Brigade. Further missions the following day hit ten armoured concentrations, 11 artillery sites and three command posts, resulting in fuel shortages for Serb mechanised units and an increasing rate of desertion. NATO officials assured reporters that the air war was ending the Serbs' ethnic cleansing activities.

The night of 11–12 May saw a peak in air action, with more than 600 sorties flown, including a decisive 'midnight' package containing B-52Hs and B-1Bs. Airfields, armament factories, bridges and air defences were among the targets. On 15 May some B-52H missions were dedicated to dropping leaflets encouraging Serb troops in Kosovo to desert before being wiped out by air attacks.

By 23 May pairs of B-52Hs, usually together with two B-1Bs, were attacking targets along the borders of Kosovo and Albania from 38,000–41,000 ft. Up to eight B-52Hs and B-1Bs launched on some of the heavier attacks. According to NATO's Combined Air Interdiction of Fielded Forces policy, Serb troops could have actually been attacked on open ground from as early as 30 March. B-52H area bombing was obviously an ideal weapon for such a task, and troop concentrations and transport were among the targets selected in the area between Prizren, in Kosovo, and Serb-held Mount Pashtrik. One of the heaviest joint raids by B-52Hs and B-1Bs from Fairford took place on 10 May when eight launched, using 'Havoc', 'Razor' and 'Titus' callsigns, and hit targets in Kosovo and Serbia.

Area attacks on ammunition dumps and airfields were also scheduled, but the Serbs were adept at dispersing and hiding ordnance. Near Sarajevo they hid 400 tons of shells in an off-limits school. Concentrations of enemy armour were also on the target list, although very few wrecked FRY tanks and AFVs were found post-war. Ten airfields were heavily bombed by B-52Hs and B-1Bs, causing significant damage.

A B-52H assault on the Serbian 549th Motorised Brigade occurred on 5 June in the Mount Pashtrik area on the Kosovo–Albania border. Another struck troop concentrations on a mountain plateau near Gorshub, where KLA units were fighting artillery and mortar duels with Serb troops. It was reported that the B-52Hs were being used to 'herd' Serb infantry into more open ground in the absence of Allied troops.

A strike by two B-52Hs and two B-1Bs on 7 June 1999, diverted from another target and coordinated with action by the KLA who were fighting Serb troops on Mount Pashtrik in Operation *Arrow*, caused severe casualties in two FRY battalions of around 1000 soldiers. Eighty-six Mk 82 bombs and dozens of CBU-87s were dropped, destroying Serb artillery ammunition and vehicles and allegedly killing around 500 troops. A further B-52H attack on the afternoon of 9 June inflicted more casualties on Serb troops. These two missions effectively ended the offensive in the area, causing ground forces to withdraw and accelerating the FRY's agreement to peace terms two days later. NATO commentators stated that the missions of 7 and 9 June were the most important attacks of the war, as they shattered Serb morale.

Air strikes continued until 10 June, when President Milošević finally realised that he was losing Russian support. He agreed to withdraw

FRY forces from Kosovo following the establishment of a UN Interim Administration Mission in the country.

On 20 June 11 B-52Hs, five B-1Bs and five KC-135Rs were still occupying Fairford's dispersal areas. However, two days later, eight of the Stratofortresses left England for Barksdale, using 'Brock' callsigns, followed by the three 5th BW examples bound for Minot as 'Hazan 12', '14' and '16'. Unlike the B-1Bs, which departed on 24 June, the B-52Hs at Fairford were rotated regularly, and between them the two types performed more than 400 sorties and delivered 11,000 Mk 82 and 20 Mk 84s bombs. Some 90 CALCMs were also launched from the Stratofortresses.

When the 93rd BS's B-52Hs returned to Barksdale, they bore numerous mission markings and nose-art. 61-0008 had 13 'tomahawk' mission markings (referring to the squadron's Indian head insignia), 60-0041 had eight and 61-0032 and 61-0022 each boasted 16.

The peace treaty signed on 3 June 1999 following OAF is often regarded as the first to be secured by air power alone. However, Serb forces within Kosovo continued to pursue a policy of wholesale destruction, while the damage to Serbia's widely dispersed military assets was later found to be less than had been originally estimated.

In the opinion of USAF Lt Gen Thomas J Keck, who was Vice Commander, HQ, ACC, during OAF, NATO air power, and particularly the B-52Hs, forced the Serbs to seek a peace deal. Bombing their troops in the open during the closing stages of the conflict compelled them to negotiate an end to the conflict. Gen Henry Shelton went further in assessing that the military and political goals of OAF had been achieved 'through a cohesive alliance of democratic nations whose military men and women conducted the most effective air campaign in history'.

Although the 72-day operation introduced new weapons, including JDAM, and revolutionary aircraft like the B-2A, the veteran B-52Hs were central to the air campaign. In 185 missions they delivered almost 9000 items of ordnance, including 6287 Mk 82 bombs, 178 750-lb M117 demolition bombs and 60 Mk 84 2000-lb weapons. Together with their cruise missiles and leaflet bombs, this comprised almost one third of the USAF's munitions delivered during OAF. As Gen Wesley Clark commented, 'To me, the jewel in the crown was when those B-52s rumbled across Kosovo'.

B-52H-175-BW 61-0039 flew OAF missions from Fairford between 24 March and 11 June 1999. The chequered fin stripe seen on the bomber was used by the 69th BS at Minot AFB at the time, but was later applied exclusively to the 5th BW flagship, 60-0005. 61-0039 dropped a number of Mk 84 bombs during several missions later in the war when conventional ordnance was used in place of CALCMs, stocks of which were running low by then (*USAF*)

## CHAPTER THREE

# MODERN WEAPONS

Many of the weapons used in *Desert Storm*, such as CALCMs and Mk 82/84 bombs were also delivered in subsequent operations over Kosovo and the extended battles in the Iraq region. One of the smallest items, the BLU-114/B 'graphite bomb', was returned to the armoury for attacks on Serb electrical transformers and powerlines in OAF. Its spools of graphite filaments were spread in a cloud by explosion, knocking out uninsulated power lines.

CALCMs, developed mainly for the B-52H and used by it in several campaigns, were usually of two kinds – AGM-86C Block 0 (2000-lb fragmentation warhead) or Block 1 (3000-lb fragmentation warhead). These warheads replaced the W80-1 nuclear-armed version fitted to the original 4450-lb AGM-86B ALCM, which had terrain contour matching guidance. The AGM-86C and AGM-86D (fitted with a 1000-lb penetrating warhead) used GPS and an inertial navigation system (INS) to locate their targets. Block 1A examples had an improved GPS receiver that was resistant to jamming. Some 1715 AGB-86Bs were produced up to 1986, while AGM-86C/D production ran to 289. A total of 200 AGM-86Bs were modified with conventional warheads at $160,000 each.

The ALCM entered service with B-52H units in August 1981, while the CALCM made its operational debut in January 1991, seeing further action in September 1996 for Operation *Desert Strike*, followed by subsequent operations. OIF I in March–April 2003 saw the first use of the AGM-86D version.

B-52H-135-BW 60-0011, complete with 'Mr Jiggs' artwork synonymous with the 11th BS flagship, is seen on the Barksdale ramp during an airshow with various combat weapons loads, including AGM-86Bs on the SUU-67/A wing pylons and snub-nosed WCMDs, a GBU-10 LGB and GBU-38 and GBU-31 JDAM on the trolleys in front of the bomber. Drag-reducing internal carriage of weapons like JASSM and JDAM has greatly improved the B-52H's range and speed (*USAF*)

Eight CALCMs are loaded onto the CSRL in a B-52H's capacious bomb-bay ahead of an OEF mission. The yellow stripe indicates a live conventional warhead (*USAF/T Panopalis Archives*)

Loading an ALCM onto a B-52 pylon required a specialised MHU-179 lift trailer, and its service introduction in front of US government dignitaries was not without incident, as Lt Col Don Campbell recalled;

'It had a hand-held control unit with a long cord so an operator could stand back and manoeuvre the trailer unit. The day before the demo, an operator screwed up and ran over the cable, crushing it. I immediately called the manufacturer in Maryland and asked if they had a spare cable. The only one available was in use on one of their own trailers, and rapid courier flights were not then available. So, they bought the cable a seat on an Empire Airlines flight and it was flown from Baltimore to Utica, New York. The next day the demo went off without a hitch.'

The 20 ft-long missile was powered by a 600-lb thrust Williams F107-WR-101 turbofan, conferring high subsonic speeds when launched from high- or low-altitudes at intervals of not less than one minute. Its wings extended to 12 ft after launch, together with extending tail surfaces and an opening engine intake, all deployed prior to the start-up of the turbofan. The ALCM had a range of more than 1500 miles (around 700 miles for an AGM-86C with a blast fragmentation warhead), allowing the B-52H to launch it from well outside defended hostile airspace.

An AGM-86C was loaded with pre-programmed mission data, as Col Floyd Carpenter explained;

'The CALCM missions were originally "built" at Offutt AFB [Nebraska] in the same system that produced the mission tapes for the ALCM [nuclear version], then transported to the unit or transmitted to our deployable mission planning system, whereupon it was converted to Data Transfer Unit Cartridges that are used in the aircraft. We took the deployable system with us to Guam and Diego Garcia, and although the original missions [in Operation *Desert Strike*] were built before we left, several changes were made and transmitted to us in Guam. In-flight changes were also made during the mission, which the navigation team had to manually input into the system.'

Before *Desert Fox* the USAF had 239 CALCMs in the inventory, 198 of them Block I and 41 Block 0 versions – 90 were fired during the campaign in December 1998. The small, low-flying air-launched cruise missile was a real challenge for Soviet air defences. A faster two-seat version of the MiG-25 'Foxbat' in the form of the MiG-31 'Foxhound' was developed specifically to counter it at low altitudes with an upgraded long-range radar.

CALCM was supposed to be replaced for the B-52H by the General Dynamics/Raytheon AGM-129A ACM – a weapon of similar size to the AGM-86, but with stealth characteristics to fool the look-down/shoot-down radars of Soviet fighters like the Su-27. Its shape comprised geometrically angular surfaces made from non-metallic materials. The swept-forward wings, lack of radar emissions and shielded jet exhaust were all intended to reduce its radar and infra-red signatures. A Williams F112-WR-100 extended its range to around 2000 miles at 500 mph with the AGM-86B's nuclear warhead. Test flights began in 1985, but financial problems saw funding for the missile terminated four years later. Although production was re-started in 1992, the end of the Cold War prompted a reduction in orders to 460 units. B-52Hs could carry 12 ACMs on external pylons and eight internally.

B-52H-155-BW 60-0050 *DRAGON'S INFERNO* from the 419th FTS releases an inert GBU-31 JDAM during a recent flight from Edwards AFB. This particular aircraft has been assigned to the AFFTC for 40 years, and in that time it has conducted test drops and launches of a variety of weapons (*USAF*)

A conventionally armed AGM-129B was requested by the USAF but cancelled in favour of the AGM-158 JASSM, and remaining stocks of AGM-129s were destroyed in 2012 to conform with the Strategic Offensive Reductions Treaty and because the missile was considered increasingly unreliable and expensive to maintain. CALCMs were phased out on 20 November 2019.

AGM-142 Have Nap/Popeye was the first PGM used by the B-52H, delivering a 750-lb blast/fragmentation or 790-lb penetrator warhead from around 60 miles' stand-off range – considerably less than a CALCM. It had either infra-red or inertial guidance. Two could be carried on the port wing pylon, with a third, and the accompanying AN/ASW-55 data-link pod, on the starboard side. It was withdrawn from use in 2003.

Initially cleared for use in the B-1B and B-2A, Boeing's JDAM became a vital addition to the B-52H's armoury from late 1997 after operational tests with a B-52H assigned to the 419th Flight Test Squadron (FTS). It was first used operationally by B-52Hs and B-1Bs in OEF in 2001. The GBU-31 version initially employed by these aircraft weighs 2000 lbs and relies on GPS-derived data to update its INS. Target coordinates are loaded into the bomb by the B-52H navigator pre-flight or during the mission. Using its own battery, the weapon powers up when selected, does its own built-in tests, aligns its INS with the B-52H's and sends a 'ready' signal to the aircraft. Nearing the target, the navigators wait until the bomb is within its Launch Acceptable Region, at which point the weapon is released. The JDAM makes its own final checks just before it leaves the aircraft.

The weapon's versatility was demonstrated during an OEF mission performed by four B-1Bs that saw 96 JDAM dropped just 20 minutes after their target had been altered mid-flight. All of the bombs' GPS coordinates had to be rapidly re-programmed within a ten-minute timeframe, each one requiring around 1500 computer keystrokes to alter its instructions.

Although the B-52H's GPS systems increased the accuracy of bombing with 'dumb' ordnance, far superior results were possible with JDAM. Initiated in 1992 by Gen Merrill McPeak and Secretary of the Air Force Donald B Rice, and in service from 1998 for both tactical and heavy bombers, the weapon was a modification kit for existing 500-lb Mk 82 up to 2000-lb Mk 84 bombs. The contract issued to Boeing called for a conversion kit to be produced (at a maximum cost of $18,000 per copy) that gave a previously 'dumb' bomb the capability of exploding within a Circular Area of Probability (CEP) of only 43 ft in all weathers. In practice, CEPs of 10–33 ft are more usual. JDAM was not originally intended for use against moving targets.

Mk 84-based JDAM contain 945 lbs of tritonal explosive with an aluminium stabiliser. When a GBU-31 explodes, 1000 lbs of steel fragments, travelling at 6000 ft per second, escape an 8500°F fireball, while the weapon makes a crater 20 ft wide. Aerodynamic control surfaces in its tail section give the bomb a range of up to 28 miles, and it is essentially a 'launch and leave' weapon.

The guidance system for the JDAM was jointly developed by the USAF and US Navy. In 2009, a Boeing laser-guided 500-lb version (GBU-54) was added using an Elbit Systems precision laser guidance set and GPS. JDAM guidance is updated continuously by GPS from the aircraft's avionics to its strap-on inertial guidance system, which takes over the task once the bomb is released. The many successful hits with 500-lb JDAM (developed from 1999) encouraged the move towards smaller, highly accurate weapons for multiple targets per sortie, which has continued since 2003.

Further JDAM developments include the winged JDAM-ER (Extended Range) glide bomb with a 45-mile range and the Powered JDAM, equipped with a small J-85 turbojet to give it a 300-mile range as a small cruise missile.

The original GBU-31 is a Mk 84 bomb with a BLU-109 penetrating warhead or BLU-117 or BLU-119 conventional warhead. The GBU-31(V)B has the KMU-559B/B tail section with moving fins, INS/GPS receiver units and battery. Lift-imparting strakes attached to the body of the bomb enable a typical range of 15 miles. The same guidance tail unit and strakes can be attached to a 1000-lb Mk 83 bomb with a BLU-110 blast-fragmentation conventional warhead to create the GBU-32 JDAM. Finally, a redesigned,

The 6 ft-wide by 28 ft-long front bomb-bay of a conventionally configured B-52H, with two of the three bomb cluster racks visible. Each rack can hold up to nine 1000-lb weapons (*Author*)

smaller KMU-572/B guidance kit can be fitted to a 500-lb bomb to make it a GBU-38/54.

JDAM and cluster munitions were used far more often in Afghan operations, where they attained exemplary accuracy, than in Kosovo. Nevertheless, in OAF, the JDAM's rate of accuracy was far higher than that of unguided Mk 82 GP bombs. Arguably, during OEF, the B-52H with JDAM was a more effective general-purpose bomber than the B-2A with similar weapons. The GBU-31 was the most commonly used JDAM variant in OIF I, where it became the second most used PGM. More than 5000 were expended, compared with 7114 GBU-12s and 153 CALCMs.

Although JDAM became the primary weapon for many B-52H missions from OEF onwards, the Raytheon Paveway series of LGBs also remains a key weapon for the bomber force. The 500-lb GBU-12 Paveway II is still in use, modified to GBU-12F or GBU-49 configuration that allows both laser and GPS guidance, while the GBU-24 Paveway III, used in Iraq and Syria, weighs 2200 lbs and offers a glide range of up to nine miles thanks to its larger wings and fins. Many have retrofitted GPS additions as Enhanced Paveway. GBU-12 was the most commonly dropped munition in OIF I, when 68 per cent of all air-delivered ordnance was guided in some way. In OEF, bad weather disturbed the guidance systems of many of the Paveway bombs.

For B-52s, it was necessary to introduce the ability to self-designate targets in the absence of ground-based target markers who were available for operations such as OEF. The USAF Weapons School conducted trials in the 1990s with B-52s using 'buddy lasing' tactics with an F-15E or F-16C equipped with a targeting pod. This led in 2003 to evaluation of the AN/AAQ-28(V) Litening II AT targeting pod, mounted on two B-52Hs. Following an accelerated development programme, three 93rd BS aircraft deployed to Fairford in April 2003 to perform operational tests of the pod some two months earlier than in the USAF's original plan. On 11 April, during OIF I, a successful attack on an Iraqi airfield was made by B-52H 61-0021, whose crew used the pod to deliver 16 CBU-103s and three GBU-12 LGBs against a command centre on Al Sahra airfield.

The integration of Litening II with the B-52H was supported by the 49th TES at Barksdale and the AFRC Test Center in Tucson, Arizona. Currently in use with 28 air forces and by nine types of aircraft within US air arms, the pod contains both short- and long-wave infra-red sensors and laser imaging so that a crew can acquire and laser-illuminate a target. For tactical aircraft, it also offers an air-to-air mode. The laser rangefinder

GBU-54 JDAM are suspended from the ejector racks on a B-52H's CRL at Al Udeid in November 2017. Upgrades to the CRL in 2019 doubled the number of munitions that could be powered up, allowing for eight to be readied for simultaneous employment. Previously, only four could be dropped and the B-52H would then have to withdraw so that the rest could be powered up for a second attack (*USAF*)

can also be used for navigation updates or to ascertain GPS coordinates for JDAM-type weapons, or even to provide targeting for other aircraft on the same mission.

Litening II's FLIR has a wide-angle search mode or a narrow acquisition and targeting view, coupled with the built-in laser rangefinder and target designator that can also be used to record imagery for bomb damage assessment (BDA). Automatic target tracking is stabilised for all tactical weapons deliveries. The AT version, introduced in 2003 and supplied to B-52H operators, also has data-link capability. Litening II's compact 7.2-ft pod, mounted on the '559 wing station' pylon beneath the right wing, is a small addition to the B-52H's starboard underwing load, but it greatly increases the aircraft's targeting capability, particularly in its multi-targeting mode in poor weather or darkness.

The Lockheed-Martin AN/AAQ-33 Sniper advanced targeting pod was tested from September 2008 and accepted for integration with the B-52H as an alternative to the Litening pod. Capable of being linked to the bomber's offensive avionics system, it can use a video downlink to transmit reconnaissance and surveillance data with video to ground forces.

Messages are written onto GBU-31(V)1/B JDAM hung on underwing racks attached to 40th AEW B-52H at Diego Garcia ahead of a March 2003 OIF I mission (*USAF/T Panopalis Archives*)

The CBU-105 Wind-Corrected Munitions Dispenser (WCMD) was designed as a cluster bomb with a Lockheed Martin tail unit kit that enabled precision delivery, compensating for wind and measuring variations in wind and atmospheric conditions during its fall. The B-52H was also specified as a carrier for the CBU-107 guided tactical munitions dispenser, loaded with 3700 metal rods capable of penetrating thick armour. Called the Passive Attack Weapon, the 1000-lb WCMD variant, produced for just four months between December 2002 and March 2003, had no explosive warhead and was specifically designed for knocking out soft-skinned targets located in unpopulated areas during OIF I.

Like JDAM, the anti-armour CBU-105 (and CBU-105B/B) Sensor Fused Weapon, developed in the 1980s for employment against massed Soviet tank formations, used GPS and INS. Its BLU-108 submunitions each held four parachute-retarded, armour-penetrating projectiles that were released at a predetermined altitude. Their infra-red sensors detected the warm metal uppersurfaces of tanks, which they attacked with armour-piercing bomblets. The WCMD sensors corrected the weapon's trajectory by measuring variations in wind and atmospheric conditions during its fall. The CBU-105 received its combat debut on 2 April 2003 in OIF I when weapons dropped from B-52H 60-0047 destroyed a large proportion of an Iraqi armoured column. Rules of Engagement (RoE) prohibited the use of CBU-105s in urban areas.

Raytheon's AGM-154 Joint Standoff Weapon (JSOW), sponsored by the Naval Air Systems Command, was developed as an unpowered 1065-lb glide bomb containing 154 combined effects bomblets. Equipped with folding wings, the JSOW has a range of up to 43 miles when dropped from 30,000 ft. In tests at Edwards AFB, California, on 8 February 2002, a B-52H successfully launched two of the weapons at two separate targets. Despite this, the USAF left the programme in 2004 in favour of developing the JASSM.

The long-range Lockheed Martin AGM-158A JASSM, initiated in 1995, was at the development and pre-production stage in 2003. Although several were supplied to the 2nd BW, they were not used during OIF I. Indeed, the weapon was not finally cleared for operational use until October 2009. Initial versions suffered from poor reliability, and this caused the project to be at risk of cancellation in 2008 – JASSM was also blighted by cost overruns. However, it was eventually accepted for service by the USAF and the air forces of Australia, Finland and Poland. Carrying a WDU-42/B 1000-lb warhead and featuring a stealthy airframe to avoid radar detection, JASSM has flip-out wings that allow it to fly for 230 miles powered by a Teledyne J402 turbojet. Guidance is inertial with GPS, and an imaging infra-red seeker is used for target recognition. The B-52H force replaced the longer-range AGM-86C/D CALCM with JASSM from 20 November 2019.

Aircrew carefully pre-flight GBU-12 Paveway II 500-lb LGBs on the internal cluster racks of a B-52H ahead of an OIF I mission in April 2003 (*USAF/T Panopalis Archives*)

An extended range version in the form of the AGM-158B JASSM-ER was purchased in 2014, improving the missile's reach to 575 miles with a similar airframe to the basic AGM-158A. B-52Hs with the 1760 Internal Weapons Bay Upgrade can carry eight JASSM-ERs internally and 12 on wing pylons. The missile was cleared for B-52H use in 2018. JASSM-XR, weighing 5000 lbs and extending the weapon's range to 1200 miles, is presently under development. Its 1000-lb penetrator warhead and stealthy airframe allow JASSM-XR to fly at higher altitudes while avoiding radar.

A more recent addition to the B-52H's arsenal is the 285-lb Boeing GBU-39/B Small Diameter Bomb. To date, the weapon had been mainly used by tactical fighters in operations against Islamic State in Syria and Iraq. Another GPS-guided glide bomb, it requires countermeasures to negate the kind of satellite signal jamming that Russia has often used against GPS-assisted weapons during its invasion of Ukraine.

## CHAPTER FOUR

# FREEDOM FROM TERRORISM

JDAM-laden B-52H-160-BW 60-0059 *THE DEVIL'S OWN*, long-standing flagship of the 96th BS, taxies out at the start of an OEF mission on 22 March 2002. Diego Garcia's lush foliage provides a distinctive background for the heavily loaded bomber. The 96th BS had been heavily involved in Operation *Anaconda*, which concluded just four days prior to this photograph being taken (*USAF/T Panopalis Archives*)

Immediately after the disastrous 11 September 2001 attack on the World Trade Centre and the Pentagon, the US government, led by President George W Bush, decided that the bases for up to 1000 of Osama bin Laden's al-Qaeda terrorists, backed by the Taliban regime in the vast and challenging terrain of eastern Afghanistan, had to be eliminated. When the Taliban refused to hand over bin Laden, the aim of the ensuing air operations became the removal of the regime and the al-Qaeda force. The latter, founded on 11 August 1988, had sheltered in Afghanistan since 1996 and carried out attacks on two US embassies in Africa and the destroyer USS *Cole* (DDG-67) in Aden prior to '9/11'. Its training camps in Afghanistan had been subjected to US cruise missile attacks in August 1998.

Eliminating al-Qaeda, or at least its 50 leaders, required long-range bombers that could deliver ordnance on landlocked targets covering large areas. The B-52 force was the most obvious weapon for the task, bombing at lower altitudes than it normally used in order to eliminate hostile forces in the open and remove Taliban air defence threats that might hinder US air superiority. These included around 50 MiG-21 and Su-22 fighters, with about 40 qualified pilots, operating from four airfields, SA-2 and SA-3 SAMs and MANPADS – amongst the latter were up to 200 US-built FIM-92 Stinger infra-red homing SAMs with a range of 12,000–15,000 ft.

Defense Secretary Donald Rumsfeld was clear that in order to 'create conditions for sustained anti-terrorist operations and humanitarian relief in Afghanistan', it would be necessary to 'remove the threat from air defences and from Taliban aircraft'. Compared with other major US operations of that period, the attrition of those air defences was fairly easily accomplished. Taliban ZSU-23/4 and 57 mm AAA could not reach the operational altitudes of the US bombers, and the few 100 mm guns in-theatre only occasionally fired shells up to about 23,000 ft if the bombers ever descended to that height.

Planners urgently sought suitable focus of the air elements required for the operation. Fairford was undergoing a major refit at the time, but the contractors accelerated the second phase of the work to allow limited bomber operations in case the base was needed after '9/11'. Instead, Diego Garcia and Guam became the focus of heavy bomber deployments, although the former location necessitated five-hour flights to Afghanistan. Stratofortresses could then remain on station over remote territory without requiring in-flight refuelling.

The 20th and 96th BSs deployed B-52Hs to Diego Garcia for OEF, personnel making do with tented accommodation as the base's population rapidly expanded. Better living quarters came with the construction of Camp Justice. The USAF also established phase inspection facilities on Guam so that the bombers no longer needed to return home for deep maintenance after each 300 flying hours period.

The *Deny Flight* operations over Iraq had already brought around 175 US aircraft to the Persian Gulf region, and two carrier battle groups were also in the area. From 19 September two USAF AEGs headed out to bases in Diego Garcia, Bahrain, Kuwait and Saudi Arabia. Diego Garcia had been made available by Great Britain in the late 1960s, and a major airfield expansion programme was undertaken by the USA. It was used by 20 B-52Gs and their tankers during the 1991 Gulf War and by B-52Hs during Operation *Desert Fox*.

Together, the bases in 2001 fielded B-52H and B-1B bombers, F-15Es, F-16Cs, tankers and E-3 AWACS aircraft. Ten B-52Hs from the 2nd and 917th Wings left Barksdale on 22 September, bound for Diego Garcia, and they were later joined by 5th BW examples and two more 20th EBS aircraft by 28 October. The bombers were assigned to the 40th AEW once in-theatre.

Most infrastructure targets were to be avoided in order to allow the impoverished Afghan nation to be reconstructed after the defeat of al-Qaeda and the Taliban. Thirty-one initial targets were chosen, including air defences and known leadership HQ buildings. The scarcity of important targets was partially due to the long period of Russian occupation, as Rumsfeld judged;

'The Soviet Union pounded it year after year. Much of the country is rubble. They do not have high-value targets that would lend themselves to substantial damage from the air.'

Gen Tommy Franks, commander of CENTCOM, which oversaw all OEF operations, warned against anticipating swift, definitive results. 'It's been said that those who expect another *Desert Storm* will wonder every day what this war is all about. This war will be fought on many fronts

A 40th AEW B-52H leaves its smoky trail to disperse in Diego Garcia's clear air on 22 October 2001 while B-1B Lancers and KC-10 Extenders await their OEF mission tasking on the flightline (*USAF/T Panopalis Archives*)

simultaneously'. Those 'fronts' included economic and political initiatives in equal measure with an air war.

The majority of tanker sessions took place off the coast of Pakistan. During their long orbits over the trouble spots, bomber crews were able to familiarise themselves with the territory and the forces on the ground who could direct their heavy weapons loads to specific targets in repeated drops. Crews with previous SAC experience soon adapted to this process, having been trained originally to dash to their Cold War targets, release ordnance and clear off as fast as possible. One mission, on 9 October 2001, hit four different targets that were considerable distances apart during a flight lasting 13 hours.

Although most missions were flown at, or occasionally below, 10,000–12,000 ft, the patrols sometimes had to orbit above cloud in the winter months, so a good understanding of the Special Operations Force's Forward Air Controllers' (FACs') requirements and instructions was vital. Throughout OEF, the air campaign relied on extensive, coordinated intelligence, surveillance and reconnaissance, precision air strikes and close cooperation with FACs on the ground. B-52Hs and 34th EBS B-1Bs (commanded by Lt Col Tom Arko) flew a higher proportion of the bombing missions in Afghanistan than they did in OAF. US Navy carrier-based jets supplied more than 70 per cent of the Tactical Air, compared with 25 per cent in OAF. In all, the hardworking Hornet pilots flying from carriers sailing in the Northern Arabian Sea flew 3700 sorties, compared with 375 by B-52H crews and six by B-2As.

Fighter-bomber crews had little time over the target for conversations with FACs, despite F-14 Tomcat and F/A-18 Hornet units flying sorties lasting more than six hours – twice their normal endurance. They also lacked available ground bases within practical striking distance of Afghan targets. When F-15Es, F-16Cs and A-10As were eventually moved to a base in Kuwait, they too had to make unusually long flights with many aerial refuellings to reach their targets. The distances also ruled out providing escort for the 'low and slow' AC-130 gunships that could loiter for nine hours, confining their valuable support to night operations. US Navy carriers were better placed geographically, albeit still at 500 miles range from target areas, and their carrier air wings were able to launch a staggering 4900 strike sorties compared with 701 by USAF heavy bombers, including 320 by the B-1B. PGMs were used in 93 per cent of their missions, including almost all the available JDAM – a B-1B's bomb-bay could hold no fewer than 24 Mk 84 JDAM.

Clearly, the B-52s and B-1Bs had the payload advantage over fighter-bombers, and 75 per cent of the munitions dropped from October 2001 to March 2002 (as the 50th anniversary of the first Stratofortress flight was about to be celebrated) came from those 'heavies'. On 2 March the 40th AEW recorded its 500th B-52H sortie when an aircraft dropped 2000-lb JDAM in eastern Afghanistan. Repeated bomb runs at a target could be made, but realigning the B-52H for a second or subsequent run could take 10–30 minutes for the necessary calculations to be made and aim points to be confirmed with CENTCOM.

OEF began on the night of 7 October with strikes on 31 selected targets by 15 B-52Hs and B-1Bs. US Navy aircraft launched from *Carl Vinson* and *Enterprise* and BGM-109 TLAMs were fired by warships – including British and American nuclear submarines that were positioned around 700 miles from their targets. For the US Navy and US Marine Corps F/A-18 Hornet and F-14 Tomcat crews who flew many of the missions, they were airborne for up to six hours, with three or four aerial refuelling sessions and less than an hour's loiter time over the target. Six carriers would ultimately participate in strikes and undertake CAS for Special Operations Forces (SOF) in Afghanistan between October 2001 and March 2002.

On the first night of OEF, airfields at Herat, Jalalabad, Kandahar and Shindand were hit (as were SAM sites at some of these locations), and F/A-18 pilots provided top cover for a JDAM attack near Jalalabad by two B-1Bs.

The heavy bomber crews had long mission times to manage during the campaign. Setting the tone for OEF on Night One, six B-52Hs of the 20th BS and 2nd and 917th Wings, together with six B-1Bs, flew 2500 miles from Diego Garcia with their maximum complements of up to 70,000 lbs of conventional Mk 82 bombs, GBU-31 JDAM or CBU-103 WCMD ordnance. Once over Afghanistan, they hit a number of air defence and command-and-control sites. Flying above the limited AAA opposition that caught the attention of US Navy aircrew in their Hornets, Tomcats and Prowlers, the Stratofortresses and Lancers delivered JDAM and WCMD for the first time.

The most punishing attacks on the first night were made by B-52Hs against nine al-Qaeda terrorist training camps in eastern Afghanistan, including one at Garmabak Ghar. However, their overall effect was somewhat reduced by the Taliban and al-Qaeda rapidly dispersing military assets and finding shelter for their principal leaders.

In the first five days of OEF, the B-52Hs and B-1Bs dropped 500 JDAM (more than half of which were expended by Lancers), 1000 Mk 82s and 50 CBU-87 cluster munitions. The CAOC managing the air war expected five B-52H sorties per day and four from B-1Bs. Both types were linked into the CAOC's communications net, which updated target information in real time and redirected bombers to new targets if necessary. It was a remarkable demonstration of the B-52H's value as a heavyweight CAS aircraft, providing essentially the same function as a tactical jet but with far greater endurance and weapons loads. Gen John Jumper, USAF Chief of Staff, described this use of the B-52 as 'transformational', pointing out that missions of this kind would usually have been flown by aircraft such as the A-10.

For B-52H crews, these long missions were exhausting. The cramped interior of the aircraft offered only one place where it was possible to stand upright – on the short ladder connecting the flightdeck and navigators'

An Afghanistan-bound B-52H meets up with its assigned KC-10 tanker in March 2002 en route to delivering its JDAM, thus underlining the tanker crews' motto – 'No-one kicks ass without tanker gas' (*USAF*)

area. The high internal noise levels ruled out normal conversation, and crews had to wear headsets throughout a flight to protect their hearing – all communication was via the intercom. Rest breaks were normally taken on the flightdeck floor. Crews usually had a day or two's break between missions.

Air superiority was achieved almost immediately with the destruction of the Taliban's limited air defences, although missions were still flown at high-altitude to mitigate any potential missile threats. In later, low-altitude attacks, B-52Hs were occasionally fired on by light Afghan AAA, but crews stayed above the guns' effective range and were usually unaware of the gunfire until they were told of it later by US ground forces. B-52Hs and B-1Bs also quickly removed the Taliban's small and largely unserviceable force of MiG-21s, Su-22s and other ex-Soviet aircraft that might have been converted into flying bombs to hit Allied bases. As Rumsfeld noted, 'The aircraft, to our knowledge, did not leave the ground'. Even disused and unserviceable aircraft were destroyed, together with their runways, command and control systems and revetments at bases like Kandahar, Shindand and Kabul.

However, the dearth of fixed targets, and the persistence and mobility of the Taliban fighters, meant that progress in eliminating the threats was slow, particularly in the southern part of Afghanistan. The Taliban proved adept at avoiding and surviving the bombing, causing some international criticism of the aerial campaign's apparent ineffectiveness.

Both the B-52H and B-1B crews provided 'on demand' CAS to Allied troops with up to five missions a day, loitering over target areas with a variety of weapons aboard. Fifteen-hour B-52H and B-1B bomber missions from Diego Garcia began with a three-hour northward flight to meet tankers off the southern Pakistani coast. They then flew to their target area, which was partly divided into Vietnam War-type 'kill boxes' later in the conflict. The missions were repeated the following day, with the same focus on command and control targets or air defence sites.

Often, a single JDAM, programmed by the B-52H navigators with coordinates received directly via a FAC's digital PRC-117 radio link, would be selected for a target while the B-52H crew flew figure-of-eight patterns and awaited instructions for another limited delivery.

In northern Afghanistan, US SOF, sometimes operating on horseback dressed as Afghans but utilising laptops or digital radios to send target coordinates to B-52s via a satellite, were inserted to fight with Northern Alliance forces. The latter was a loose aggregation of tribes that became the principal Afghan internal opposition to the Taliban. The pace of air strikes had increased during October, and it culminated the following month with intensive bombing around the northern city of Mazar-i-Sharif. This allowed Afghan fighters with the Northern Alliance (some of them also on horseback) to drive the enemy from the outskirts of the city. Further B-52H strikes opened the way for its capture in November, which was seen as a turning point in the war.

By then, the loitering bomber 'cells' of aircraft above Taliban forces would include three or more B-52Hs and a B-1B, awaiting FAC instructions. Coordinated bomb drops by all aircraft in the cell ploughed up large areas of arid terrain. SOF frequently provided data to enable a B-52H crew to drop a load of ordnance within an *Arc Light*-type 3000-ft 'kill box'. With finer adjustment, on one occasion a bridge that Taliban fighters were about to cross was destroyed by three direct hits from JDAM.

After dealing with a number of single, both pre-planned targets, including additional terrorist camps, during the first week of the conflict, the focus for bomber crews moved to a mixture of both pre-planned and 'flexible', or 'time-critical', targets so that pilots would take off not knowing what targets they would be told to attack. 'Flex' targets might reveal themselves through electronic emissions, movement out of cover or intercepted communications, bringing down the 'Damoclean sword' from a patrolling B-52H.

Stratofortresses participated in a key mission on 19 October following the early attempts to insert SOF into the mountainous areas of northern Afghanistan. FACs were emplaced ahead of helicopter insertion, and a B-52H was directed to take out a Taliban bunker near Mazar-i-Sharif.

From 21 October, the Stratofortress missions tended towards CAS, managed by ground-based USAF FACs or Joint Terminal Attack Controllers (JTACs) working with around 300 SOF troops to provide targeting coordinates. 'Carpet bombing' missions against entrenched positions north of Kabul and around Bagram air base were intended to degrade Taliban forces ahead of operations by Allied ground troops. In all cases, securing target approval was a complex business that sometimes slowed down the progress of the campaign. The result was usually the same – hard-bitten Taliban forces sustained heavy casualties and then abandoned their positions after a B-52H strike.

In one notable mission the crew of B-52H 60-0022 saved the life of a FAC who was being pursued and fired at by Taliban. Having resolved some inaccurately delivered coordinates, the crew dropped JDAM on Taliban positions and followed up with a pinpoint attack on a Taliban commander in his bunker nearby. They then destroyed a substantial number of Taliban cavalry who were blocking a Northern Alliance attack on Mazar-i-Sharif.

On 31 October the DoD stated that B-52Hs had begun 'carpet bombing' Taliban lines 15 miles north of Kabul, and that 3000 weapons had been delivered by then. Throughout November it was usual to have four or five B-52Hs and a B-1B on station over a target area at any one time.

The flexibility, endurance and ordnance capacity of the big bombers made them more useful in many Afghan situations than tactical fighter-bombers, as Maj Gen Walter Buchanan, Deputy Chief of Staff for Air and Space Operations, HQ, USAF, observed. 'The bomber brings lots of muscle to the fight because of its long loiter time above the target and high payload carrying 24 JDAM, or more, as opposed to fighters going in with, typically, four JDAM and not nearly as much loiter time'.

Accurate target information was occasionally too hard to obtain and errors did occur. On 26 October two B-52Hs and a pair of F/A-18Cs inadvertently bombed a warehouse in Kabul that was thought to be a Taliban HQ. It was actually in use by the International Red Cross as a storage facility for humanitarian relief, which meant that it should have been removed from the CENTCOM target list. Sadly, a second attack was also carried out despite the warehouse having a Red Cross emblem painted on its roof. The Pentagon described the attack as 'a human error in targeting procedure'.

Another tragic error occurred on 1 July 2002, some months after the main bombing campaign had ended and air power was being used to protect US ground troops who had entered the country. An Afghan wedding party was hit and 40 civilians died. The strike was initially attributed to a stray JDAM from a B-52H that was bombing caves in the same area. Eventually, it was established that an AC-130 gunship crew had attacked the party after they thought that celebratory rifle fire into the air by the guests had been sustained AAA aimed at them.

For targets of opportunity on the battlefield, some of them elusive or only briefly available, the lack of exact GPS coordinates from FACs or laser designation of a target by a ground-based operator sometimes meant that rapid decisions had to be made, resulting in occasional mis-targeting. The US Navy Hornet pilots who often hit similar targets to B-52H crews tended to use 'dumb' bombs, as they could be dropped without taking the time to set up laser or GPS targeting and run the risk of missing targets that were briefly available.

However, the B-52's traditional role as a heavy bomb 'truck' was also employed throughout OEF. This capability was adapted through 'flexible targeting' – a skill which B-52 and B-1B crews had been developing in the two years prior to the commencement of Afghan operations. The scarcity of important fixed targets made this ability to respond rapidly to emerging or mobile targets of opportunity vital. The technique could include target information being supplied by other aircraft. Sometimes, B-52H crews would receive target coordinates from US Navy fighter-bomber crews, relayed via an AWACS aircraft.

A perfect example of 'flexible targeting' came on 12 November 2001, when a SOF FAC called in a B-52H to drop its 45 Mk 82 'dumb' bombs on a large Taliban force that was gathering to attack Bagram airfield – a vital base that had only fallen to the Royal Navy's Special Boat Squadron two days earlier. The attempt to recapture the airfield was duly driven off.

For precise hits on smaller targets, the more costly JDAM was preferred. FACs with GPS devices radioed the target coordinates to the bomber crew, who then programmed the weapon accordingly. These ground teams evolved a target selection package that included a laser range finder, GPS, thermal imaging sight (for night use), satellite radio transmitter and a standard lap-top computer. This relatively simple package was capable of establishing target coordinates within a few feet and rapidly transmitting them to a loitering bomber crew so that full clearance to attack often took less than 30 minutes.

Planned missions could sometimes by diverted to provide relief for US ground forces who were under attack by Taliban and al-Qaeda fighters. The tactics required of B-52 crews were very different from anything they had been trained for, and they quickly learned the skills needed for 'on-call' CAS, rather than high-altitude straight-and-level, single pass strategic bombing. Those attacks could be made at lower altitudes, although the Taliban were known to have some small calibre anti-aircraft weapons and MANPADS.

Northern Alliance morale was raised by the sight of a distant B-52H circling at high altitude and overflying known Taliban positions several times, with ineffective AAA attempting to reach the aircraft, before releasing its bomb load. Afghan fighters, who had previously been opposed to the heavy bombing because they feared being mistakenly attacked by high-flying USAF aircraft, would then see a long strip of territory erupt with explosions, accompanied by cheers from the Northern Alliance troops. The provision of expert SOF FACs greatly reduced the risk of inaccurate bombing with Mk 82s, which had previously been limited to *Arc Light*-type area bombing strikes some distance from the frontline for fear of causing collateral damage to friendly forces.

M117s are carefully attached to the bomb-bay racks of a B-52H at Diego Garcia, the weapons being expertly lifted into position by an armourer at the wheel of an MJ-1 loader. Nicknamed the 'jammer' by USAF personnel, the purpose-built MJ-1 has been the bomb load vehicle of choice since the 1950s. Fitted with a 25 hp engine that powers the drive wheels and cantilever lift arm, the 'jammer' can handle ordnance up to a weight of 3000 lbs (*USAF*)

There were no such concerns with JDAM, however, with one B-52H attack in the Tora Bora region seeing a GBU-31 dropped within 1500 yards of a SOF position following guidance by a FAC.

Reflecting the range of targets that could be hit during the course of one mission, on 1 November a B-52H attack on the town of Qara Bagh at midday saw three bombs destroy a Taliban base and start an intense fire. The same aircraft then went on to bomb a Taliban tank and artillery pieces on Totah Khan mountain. On advice from Northern Alliance commanders, the B-52Hs subsequently bombed Taliban forces in their defensive trenches where many had gathered to resist an advance on Kabul that had been delayed by a shortage of fuel and ammunition. The Stratofortresses then struck a fuel and ammunition store north of Kabul and a Taliban garrison in northern Takhar Province, while additional bombing near Bagram broke up Taliban positions that controlled the road into Kabul.

The type of ordnance being used by the B-52H in OEF soon extended beyond the preferred JDAM and Mk 82 'dumb' bombs – the latter caused many casualties among Taliban fighters caught out on open ground. CBU-103 WCMD GPS-guided cluster bombs, which could be delivered from higher altitudes than standard types of CBU, made their combat debut on 20 October 2001, and 450 had been dropped by the end of November, often followed up by Mk 82s. In the opening week of OEF, more than 80 per cent of the bombs dropped on Taliban targets, including 500 LGBs, 1000 Mk 82s and 50 CBUs, came from USAF bombers, which provided 40 per cent of the strike sorties in total. Typical B-52H loads early in the campaign were 12 JDAM and 27 Mk 82s, followed by 16 CBU-103 or CBU-87 WCMDs and 27 Mk 82s from late October.

Although B-52Hs were responsible for only ten per cent of the 7100 USAF sorties flown by 17 December, they delivered 70 per cent of the ordnance. Carrier-borne and US Marine Corps fighter-bombers used LGBs initially, delivering 300 in the first week, after which 'dumb' bombs were introduced. Tomcats and Hornets eventually delivered more than 35 per cent of the ordnance dropped in OEF, despite flying just three per cent of the total bombing sorties undertaken. More than half the weapons dropped by 10 December were 'smart', including GBU-10s from B-52Hs.

The aircraft's long endurance and extensive weapons load, together with the neutralisation of most Taliban air defences, allowed Stratofortresses to orbit freely over much of Afghanistan, making numerous passes on targets as soon as they received new coordinates from a FAC. Importantly, the CAOC at Prince Sultan Air Base, Saudi Arabia, which was the nerve centre of all US operations in the region, also ensured that no friendly aircraft or troops were situated below the B-52Hs' 39,000-ft bombing altitude. Each target received a few selected weapons, and on some occasions a crew found their own targets using FLIR or even binoculars when flying at lower altitudes. For missions like these, where pilots communicated directly with FACs, navigators chose and prepared the weapons and direction of attack and the B-52H crews received BDA directly from the FAC.

These were completely new tactics for Stratofortress crews, and very different from the types of Cold War missions they had flown with SAC. Together with the use of far more PGMs, such tactics also markedly reduced the numbers of aircraft, ordnance items and missions required compared with the types of B-52 missions flown against pre-planned targets in previous campaigns like *Desert Storm*. OEF required only 20 per cent of the mission totals generated for OAF, when NATO was flying 300 strike missions each day in the latter stages of the 11-week operation. For OEF, many B-52H mission generated only two aircraft.

Also, there were far fewer 'static' targets to hit than there had been in the Balkans. Taliban and al-Qaeda forces kept on the move, and targets would emerge only when detected by ground troops or FACs. Fast action and appropriate ordnance were then needed from loitering B-52Hs. Sometimes, these requirements meant that crews would fly 4000 miles to the target area, loiter until their fuel limits were reached, and then return without being given targets. However, their presence was invariably noted by terrorists whose activities may well have been limited by the threat from above, indicated by the B-52Hs' distinctive contrails as they orbited high above.

In preparation for nocturnal missions, Stratofortress crews had received training in the use of night-vision goggles, and their aircraft had the Combat Track II data link system. When flying at night, the B-52H cockpit was usually lit by red ambient lighting. A simpler version of the Joint Tactical Information Display System, Link 16 was widely used by the DoD throughout the US armed forces. It allowed mission planners to supply or change target information, or revise mission profiles, in flight via communication with the CAOC. Link 16 could also provide re-programming for JDAM via a keypad. To make the most of this innovation, RoE in OEF was quickly adapted to prioritise CAS, although B-52H crews had to be able to identify their new targets positively before attacking them. This sometimes meant that they had to haul a number of their 'dumb' bombs back to Diego Garcia, and it underlined the need for a Sniper-type pod to facilitate self-targeting.

By late 2001, 'flex' targets accounted for more than 80 per cent of the ordnance dropped in Afghanistan, their coordinates being supplied to bomber crews while they approached the target areas or loitered above them. 'Flex' targets could include moving vehicles or armour, in which case timely permission for weapons release was sometimes too difficult to secure. One or two might be hit by ordnance dropped from a fighter-bomber, which would then have to return to base immediately. However, a B-52H or B-1B could orbit over potential target areas for hours thanks to their range and weapons capacity, allowing crews to respond to a FAC's requirements with a variety of ordnance depending on the situation. Single point targets could be destroyed by a solitary JDAM, trench areas attacked with a string of Mk 82s or Mk 84s and buildings or hardened targets hit with BLU-109/B 2000-lb penetrators – all on the same mission.

Hundreds of Taliban fighters were killed by two massive 15,000-lb BLU-82/B Ammonal 'Daisy Cutters' dropped from *Combat Talon* MC-130Es near the village of Aq Kupruk on 5 November. These weapons were expended in support of 8000 Allied and Afghan Uzbek forces, the latter led by Gen Abdul Dostum, who, following an uneasy alliance with Tajik and Hazara forces, conducted a two-prong assault on Taliban-held Mazar-e-Sharif. Directed by a SOF unit, 'Tiger 2' (three-ship flights of B-52Hs and lone Predator UAV drones) was used in determined direct attacks on the enemy following the 'Daisy Cutter' drops.

Three days earlier, B-52Hs had dropped CBUs and 'carpet bombed' Taliban forces on the approaches to Mazar-e Sharif. Rather than Vietnam-style 'Arc Light' carpet bombing, where an entire strip of terrain several miles long could be virtually obliterated by a cell of B-52s, the introduction of PGMs meant that each bomb in a substantial load could be individually targeted. An early example of such an attack occurred on 31 October, when 61 aircraft, including 50 US Navy fighter-bombers, participated in saturation bombing. The following day, B-52Hs knocked out the power station supplying electricity to Taliban-occupied Kandahar.

The continuous bombing of Taliban defensive positions surrounding Mazar-e Sharif through 5 November allowed Dostum to undertake a series of advances on the city. The enemy's defensive trenches were repeatedly bombed, with heavy casualties, although more troops were soon sent to fill the gaps, and they too were bombed. Taliban commander Mullah Razzak was killed by a bomb on 8 November near Mazar-i-Sharif, and the next day B-52Hs targeted the Tangi gap, which formed an entrance to the city. Many of Dostum's men were almost lost, however, when they prematurely advanced into a barrage of LGBs from F/A-18C Hornets.

Finally, on 10 November, the Northern Alliance secured the first important victory against the Taliban when it broke through enemy lines and took Mazar-i-Sharif. Taliban spokesmen said they had been forced out by the heavy US bombing. Large numbers of fighters had defected or tried to join the opposition. To many observers, the defeat of the Taliban and al-Qaeda in Afghanistan by air power overturned traditional beliefs in the need for a land war, particularly as so few bombers were actually used at any one point. Just ten B-52Hs and eight B-1Bs were involved, together with 12 sorties by six of Whiteman's B-2As. Together, they delivered 76 per cent of the aerial ordnance in only a fifth of the total combat missions flown during the first three weeks of the war. The B-52H element accounted for 584 sorties and 13 million pounds of ordnance.

A Pentagon briefing session for the press during November included film of the devastating effects of a B-52H strike on the enemy's fielded forces as evidence of the undermining of Taliban control by bombing.

Early that same month, the CAOC received a request for assistance, and a B-52H delivered ordnance on target within 20 minutes of the alert being raised. In another incident, Northern Alliance troops on horseback led by Gen Dostum detected a heavily armed Taliban outpost containing a tank and numerous troops near Kunduz and asked for an air strike on it, assuming that this would take several days to organise. The SOF JTAC with the group recorded the coordinates with a portable digital map display and laser range finder and transmitted them to the CAOC. A loitering B-52H obliterated the target with 16 CBUs within 19 minutes of the CAOC receiving the request.

With air support of this order, Northern Alliance forces were emboldened to re-take a number of towns and villages from Taliban control. During one 93rd BS night mission, a B-52H crew orbited for three hours while an F-16C and then an A-10A attempted to identify a specified target. It was finally obliterated by an AC-130 Spectre gunship just as the B-52H crew were preparing their attack.

There were occasional errors in targeting, but effective FAC was a crucial element in the operation and it did prevent many potential tragedies. US Navy SEAL observers in a target area were able to abort a B-52H attack on a group of Taliban when they noticed women and children within their ranks. Link 16 wideband data link was a reliable means of receiving updated information, but it was not available in all aircraft. Heavy bomber crews could often receive approved target coordinates through e-mail and respond immediately.

By 12 November Allied forces were ready to dislodge the Taliban from the Afghan capital, Kabul. A series of heavy B-52H attacks on defensive lines around the city preceded an armoured advance that drove the Taliban out of Kabul and killed Mohammed Atef, Osama bin Laden's deputy. Rumsfeld announced that 'the targeting and effectiveness [of the air attacks] has improved, and that has clearly played a part in killing Taliban and al-Qaeda troops'.

President Bush also highlighted the achievements of the air war, stating 'it has been a proving ground' that has 'shown that an innovative doctrine and high-tech weaponry can shape and then dominate an unconventional conflict'. The combination of 'real-time intelligence, local Allied forces,

SOF and precision air power has really never been used before. The conflict in Afghanistan has taught us more about the future of our military than a decade of blue-ribbon panels and think-tank symposiums'.

The last major Taliban stronghold at Kunduz was subjected to 11 days of heavy bombing by B-52Hs in November in the hope that the enemy might be persuaded to surrender. Some 12 tanks and 50 other vehicles were destroyed, together with more than 40 bunkers, forcing the Taliban to capitulate to avoid further heavy bombing. Their initial failure to do so as they dug in for prolonged resistance prompted a three-pronged Northern Alliance attack, defeating them five days later. Thereafter, B-52Hs were given orbits over potential targets south of Kunduz, helping to drive Taliban elements progressively out of Bamyan, Herat, Jalalabad and, finally, Kandahar, where Taliban forces made their last stand before surrendering on 23 November.

However, several thousand surviving al-Qaeda and Taliban fighters regrouped in the Tora Bora mountains and infiltrated Kandahar. More than 1000 al-Qaeda personnel, allegedly including bin Laden himself, were suspected of hiding in the massive Tora Bora caves complex in the 14,000-ft Spin Ghar mountain range in southeast Afghanistan on the border with Pakistan. Tunnels extended more than 1000 ft into the mountains led to 200 caves and heated, air-conditioned, artificially lit chambers where large stores of weapons were hidden beyond the reach of even the B-52H's 'bunker buster' bombs.

Surveillance teams detected large numbers of well-armed al-Qaeda fighters there, and they became a target for three weeks of intensive bombing by the B-52Hs, B-1Bs and long-range F-14 Tomcats from the beginning of OEF through to year-end. Cave entrances became feasible targets. One was destroyed by an AGM-142 Have Nap missile with a rock-penetrating warhead flown into its entrance from a B-52H, and followed by a BLU-82/B dropped from a *Combat Talon* MC-130E that collapsed another cave refuge where al-Qaeda leaders were thought to be hiding. Three more B-52Hs continued the assault an hour later, causing massive rock-slides and a secondary explosion that sent smoke spiralling more than 5000 ft into the air.

B-52Hs were called in to intensify bombing of the caves complexes from 12 November. The potential problems associated with using ground-based JTACs were highlighted on 5 December when an inexperienced controller called in a B-52H to bomb a small group of Taliban 1000 m from where he was hiding. He inadvertently supplied his own GPS coordinates to the crew. When the bomber's navigators asked for confirmation, since the

B-52H-135-BW 60-0001 *Memphis Belle IV* displays its very full OEF mission scoreboard as B-52H-160-BW 60-0058 *WAR HOG* approaches Diego Garcia's long runway to signal the end of a mission. During *Memphis Belle IV*'s deployment to the atoll in 2002, Col Chris Patterson, 40th AEW commander, presented the crew of the veteran bomber with a cake to celebrate the first B-52 flight some 50 years previously on 15 April 1952 (*USAF*)

designated position had previously been marked as 'friendly', the reading was confirmed by the controller and a single 2000-lb GBU-31 exploded on Northern Alliance forces. Three US troops and five Afghans were killed, and future Afghan president, Hamid Karzai, visiting the area at the time, was slightly injured. Later, it was established that the JTAC's GPS receiver had just been connected to a new battery pack, and no allowance had been made for the device automatically reverting to its own coordinates in that situation.

An easier kill occurred on 1 December when a 93rd BS crew delivered Mk 82s and CBU-103s on Taliban fighters who were firing MANPADS at US Navy F-14s that were attacking them with LGBs. Despite bombing from around 38,000 ft, the B-52H eliminated the missile threat.

On 12 December al-Qaeda fighters in the Tora Bora mountains failed to respond to an invitation to surrender, resulting in a resumption of heavy bombing by B-52Hs, which had been pounding the area for the previous nine days. Bombing was suspended again on 18 December, with Taliban rule having been effectively ended by that time after Kandahar was finally cleared of hostile elements nine days earlier. B-52H patrols over the area continued for a week, without crews dropping any ordnance.

The most intensive use of air power in OEF was from October 2001 to January 2002, but the numbers of sorties flown was still well below that of OAF. A scarcity of targets and the lack of air bases close to Afghanistan contributed to this, but the increased versatility of the available air assets, particularly in tackling 'flex' targets or performing on-call CAS, compensated for a lack of numbers. More than 1000 PGMs were dropped during 100 daily missions by bombers and tactical aircraft, including JDAM from B-52Hs to cause landslides and bury Taliban equipment, including a tank.

Despite the intense bombing of Tora Bora, bin Laden and around 800 of his followers escaped to Pakistan, assisted by bribed local militia, on around 17 December, leaving behind large supplies of weapons in the caves. Some survivors were traced to caves in Zhawar Kili in eastern Afghanistan, where they were subjected to four more days of bombing by B-52Hs, B-1Bs and F/A-18Cs from 3 January 2002. In one attack, four Lancers sealed off a cave complex at Zhawar Kili with JDAM. Eventually, all the caves over an area of three square miles were made inaccessible by bombing and rock-slides. Large quantities of weapons and ammunition were also destroyed by US Navy SEALs and several tanks and AAA pieces were eliminated during the bombing.

Although the Bonn Conference established Hamid Karzai as president of Afghanistan in December 2001, the threat of Taliban resurgence remained. The country's severely damaged infrastructure and lack of facilities for air assets precluded tactical aircraft from operating within the country until suitable bases had been built. Reaching targets in the area required numerous inflight refuelling sessions for each sortie by a fighter-bomber, allowing such aircraft only a few minutes over the target. The Diego Garcia bomber force therefore had to remain on duty, flying daily combat patrols over Afghanistan for four more years. For these missions, B-52Hs needed all 10,000 ft of the island's runway to get airborne with heavy fuel and weapons loads.

Further B-52H attacks on cave complexes in the Paktia and Kandahar provinces occurred. Together with B-1Bs using F-16Cs to provide targeting for JDAM on at least one occasion, plus F/A-18Cs and an AC-130 gunship, they made 188 strikes on tunnels and cave refuges for terrorists in the borderlands area with Pakistan.

On 2 March 2002, B-52Hs were also called in to make the first attacks in Operation *Anaconda*, which saw US ground troops introduced in an attempt to surround and crush the remaining Taliban and al-Qaeda forces that were regrouping at Gardez, in the small Shah-i-Kot Valley in eastern Afghanistan. US SOF, commanded by Maj Gen Franklin L 'Buster' Hagenback, were directly involved for the first time against unexpectedly large enemy forces in prepared ambush positions. They suffered eight losses in the biggest battle of the Afghan campaign, which lasted for 17 days until 18 March. Working with somewhat unreliable local militia, SOF was tasked with dislodging about 1000 well-equipped al-Qaeda fighters from the valley and a mountain ridgeline near Gardez.

Air power was not at first effectively integrated with the ground advances, but in a decisive 18-hour battle, an initial B-1B attack was thwarted by a hung bomb and confused instructions that caused a follow-up F-15E Strike Eagle attack to be called off. An AC-130U Spectre gunship inadvertently strafed loyal Afghan troops during the operation due to a navigational error. As the sustained al-Qaeda mortar fire continued, a B-52H from Diego Garcia finally bombed the main enemy troop concentration, allowing the wounded Afghan troops to be airlifted out while an AC-130U dealt with the remaining hostile groups.

By 2 March, the B-52Hs of the 20th EBS/40th AEW had flown 500 Afghan missions, more than in *Desert Storm*, delivering 6500 tons of ordnance. However, substantial numbers of al-Qaeda remained in the area, and American losses occurred on 4 March when a US Army Chinook helicopter carrying a SEAL team was hit by a rocket-propelled grenade. One of the SEALs, PO1C Neil Roberts, was executed by al-Qaeda troops after being captured.

Tactical fighter-bombers attacked the 700 terrorists who emerged from caves around 'Roberts Ridge', and a B-52H was called in to drop JDAM. As the operation built up, more Stratofortresses bombed the ridge from 39,000ft, while B-1Bs and tactical fighter-bombers delivered their ordnance from 22,000–25,000ft in a scenario that required exact timing and deconfliction. In the latter stages of the conflict, more than over 80 per cent of the targets for Allied aircrew were not pre-planned. During *Anaconda*, 18 SOF teams, each of 12 men, located and marked the targets with hand-held laser markers, transmitting the information to incoming jets as required.

In subsequent *Anaconda* missions, F-15Es, A-10As and helicopter gunships sometimes had to disengage from their mountain-top targets due to unexpectedly heavy AAA, which badly damaged five 101st Aviation Regiment AH-64 Apaches engaging al-Qaeda insurgents who had surrounded hundreds of US troops. B-52Hs bombing from 39,000 ft and B-1Bs and fighter-bombers delivering their ordnance from 25,000 ft were urgently called in to hit the enemy with JDAM and LGBs. The lower-flying jets risked aerial collision over the confined battlefield and bombs

LGB-armed F-14A 'Nickel 100' (BuNo 159428) of VF-211, embarked in USS *John C Stennis* (CVN-74), flies in formation at high altitude with B-52H-165-BW 61-0004 of the 23rd BS/5th BW, forward-deployed to Diego Garcia from Minot AFB, shortly after *Anaconda*. Ten Stratofortresses were based on the atoll in the Indian Ocean from the very start of OEF and, typically, five B-52H sorties would be generated per day to Afghanistan. 61-0004 carries multiple JDAM on its inner wing racks (*Lt(jg) Mitch McCallister*)

Access to tankers has always been essential for Stratofortress operations, and this was particularly the case during the long-range missions synonymous with OEF – typically a B-52H would be airborne for more than 12 hours when flying missions over Afghanistan from Diego Garcia. Here, 2nd BW flagship B-52H-135-BW 60-0002 *SPIRIT OF BOSSIER & SHREVEPORT* receives fuel from 60th AMW KC-10A Extender 83-0076. KC-10As flew their last combat mission on 5 October 2023, being replaced by the KC-46 Pegasus (*USAF/T Panopalis Archives*)

from the B-52Hs above them as they strafed the al-Qaeda force.

Most of the enemy's estimated 300 casualties were caused by the 751 bombs dropped during the first three days of *Anaconda* (averaging 100 tons daily, almost all from B-52Hs and B-1Bs), but the operation was later criticised for the lack of coordination between ground and air assets. As the engagement became more prolonged, further units were brought in to launch attacks in the crowded airspace above the Shah-i-Kot Valley, including night-capable A-10As from Kuwait, F-16Cs, French Mirage 2000Ds and US Marine Corps AH-1W SuperCobras. From high above, the B-52Hs continued to target and destroy individual gun and mortar positions as requested by JTACs.

The determined al-Qaeda resistance was ended on 11 March by a tank assault, although more than half the insurgents escaped into the mountains. US Navy SEAL teams continued to hunt both them and sympathetic parties of Chechen mercenaries.

During *Anaconda*, around 58 per cent of the munitions used against enemy targets came from B-52Hs of the 20th EBS (led by Lt Col Paul G 'Taco' Bell), which was part of the 40th AEW, commanded by Col Chris Patterson. B-1B units in-theatre were assigned to the 28th AEW, led by Col Edward Rice, with command of the OEF tasking being shared equally between B-52H and B-1B personnel. Deployments to Andersen were made roughly every two years from 2004 to 2011. Until early 2007, B-52Hs would fly missions from Guam lasting 18 hours to reach targets in southern Afghanistan.

Although the Taliban were removed from power, mainly through the 6500 sorties flown by US aircraft, including B-52Hs, many of the al-Qaeda elements escaped to Pakistan and were soon ready to foment further discontent. The deployed B-52H forces delivered a substantial proportion of the 22,000 munitions dropped by air, 60 per cent of which were PGMs.

The Taliban insurgency in Afghanistan resumed towards the end of 2005, when its leaders, very few of whom had been killed in the fighting of 2001–02, returned from their refuges in Pakistan and organised sabotage of the provisional government, which had been elected into office in 2004. Diego Garcia-based B-52Hs joined USAF F-15Es, A-10As and RAF Harrier GR 7s in Operation *Mountain Lion* – a major effort to suppress Taliban activity in the Kunar Province – from 11 April 2006. The air strikes were better coordinated with the US Army's 10th Mountain Division, the 3rd Marine Division of the US Marine Corps and the Afghan National Army than they had been in Operation *Anaconda*. In one mission, five al-Qaeda leaders were killed. Up to 16 CAS missions were flown daily, increasingly involving the 9th EBS's upgraded B-1Bs from 6 May, dropping various types of PGM.

The Taliban's sources of wealth were selected as a primary means of undermining their power in the country. Operation *Jagged Knife* in 2017–18 was aimed at their $200 m per annum opium industry – a main source of income to fund terrorist recruitment and weapons. It involved B-52H raids on 25 drug factories, including one in Musa Qala that was hit by a 2000-lb bomb. Ten drug production facilities were hit on the first night of the operation.

*Jagged Knife* also saw the first combat missions flown in Afghanistan by 27th FS F-22A Raptors, using small-diameter 250-lb GBU-39/B bombs. They also escorted B-52Hs from the 69th EBS/379th AEW, which flew from Al Udeid, where they had been based since 2016 (B-1Bs had used the facility since the summer of 2006, rather than Diego Garcia) after its taxiways had been widened to allow for the bomber's wingspan and outrigger wheels. While deployed to Al Udeid, the 69th EBS's B-52Hs achieved a world record by dropping 24 PGMs on Taliban forces in a single mission.

Arrangements to withdraw US forces had begun under President Barack Obama in May 2014. Two presidents later, negotiations with the Taliban initiated by President Donald Trump led to an announcement by President Joe Biden of a full withdrawal by September 2021. This operation, begun as the Taliban were already moving to reoccupy the country, was covered by six 23rd BS B-52Hs flying from Al Udeid. However, their missions were mainly intended to provide tactical information and coverage for Afghan troops, as well as protecting the remaining Coalition forces as they headed out of a very long war. As before, patrols over territory threatened by the Taliban could last up to 22 hours, and in all, 240 more sorties were flown by the end of OEF on 30 August 2021.

Fuel streaks along its fuselage shows that this JDAM-laden 2nd BW B-52H has just topped off its capacious tanks during a February 2006 OEF mission, flown by Capt Will Byers and Maj Tom Aranda. Raised projections on top of the fuselage house (from front to rear) AN/ARC-19 Satellite communications equipment, GPS and AN/ARR-85 transverse magnetic antennas. AN/ARC-210 radio and AN/ALQ-122 Smart Noise Operation Equipment long-range radar jammer antennas can be seen just forward of the tail (*USAF*)

## CHAPTER FIVE

# FREE IRAQ

Unmarked 40th AEW B-52H-140-BW 60-0019 hauls a load of JDAM aloft for an OIF I sortie from Diego Garcia on 2 April 2003. It was one of 14 Stratofortresses based on the atoll during the campaign (*USAF/T Panopalis Archives*)

America and its Coalition allies have been involved in the use of air power in the attempt to resolve conflicts in Iraq for more than 30 years. At the centre of that confrontation in the late 1990s lay Saddam Hussein's consistent opposition to UN resolutions and attempts to monitor his weapons programmes for more than ten years following the end of *Desert Storm* in February 1991. This finally produced a decisive reaction from a US administration that had been horrified by the attacks on 11 September 2001, the latter considerably hardening US policies regarding potential sources of terrorism.

Within a week of the destruction of the World Trade Center and the damage inflicted on the Pentagon, President Bush had initiated plans for offensives in both Afghanistan and Iraq to frustrate future attempts at similar terrorist destruction. Subsequent military action in Iraq has required several major air campaigns, including OIF I, which would involve 28 B-52Hs flying from two bases. Despite these efforts by America and its allies, the various rival groups involved in pursuing civil disorder in the Iraq region continue their struggles for power after three decades of near-constant fighting.

OIF I, occurring only a year after OEF had seemingly reached an end in Afghanistan, had the clear objectives of regime change in Iraq, removal of the country's presumed nuclear and biological WMD and the neutralisation of associated terrorist groups in the area, with the overall aim

## CHAPTER FIVE  FREE IRAQ

of building a 'stable nation'. A short but decisive air campaign, using the full range of Coalition assets, including heavy bombers, was to be followed by a 'blitzkrieg' land operation by the US Army, US Marine Corps, British and Australian forces, as well as other Coalition members.

The opening 'Shock and Awe' air assault, technically known as Effects Based Targeting, was designed to cause a rapid change in the adversary's behaviour, ideally resulting in a rapid surrender with a minimum level of civilian casualties and damage. Precision strikes were therefore an essential part of the strategy adopted by Gen Tommy Franks, Commander-in-Chief, CENTCOM.

Saddam Hussein had dealt only with aerial attacks from the Coalition in previous campaigns, and his forces did not expect a land assault too. He felt that he had survived *Desert Storm*, which had driven his forces out of Kuwait without Coalition troops entering Iraq, and he did not believe that the US public would tolerate another war in Iraq, allowing him to remain in power indefinitely. The Iraqi president also thought that opposition from Russia and France would prevent a US invasion.

However, for the US and other Coalition members, the removal of Saddam Hussein was seen to be necessary, both to negate the risk that he might use WMD against neighbours and to demonstrate to other sponsors of terrorism that severe consequences would result from the kind of intransigence that Iraq had shown to the world. The consequent war, intended to liberate rather than defeat Iraq, and its aftermath became highly controversial, but the three-week-long OIF I was also widely regarded as an outstanding example of the well-coordinated use of combined forces.

During March–April 2003, air operations against Saddam Hussein's regime resumed in earnest. Amongst earlier actions, an attack on 13 January by 114 aircraft on Iraqi air defences was followed by a second five days later involving 29 F-15E Strike Eagles and RAF Tornado GR 4s.

From 19 March all three of the ACC's heavy bombers demonstrated successes that would make defence planners re-evaluate the bomber's place within the USAF's 21st century assets. The availability of more types of PGMs meant that air attacks could concentrate on specific objectives that would undermine Iraq's Ba'athist leadership rather than causing the widespread destruction of the country's infrastructure wrought in *Desert Storm*. ACC's B-52H, B-1B and B-2A fitted well into this policy.

On 21 March 2003 Minot-based 23rd BS B-52H-160-BW 60-0060 *IRON Butterfly* was among the first Stratofortresses to arrive at Fairford for OIF I. It subsequently led the opening B-52H attack of the campaign as 'Dogleg 25', commanded by Capt Jason D Horton, after Lt Col Robert Bussian, the squadron commander, had to abort his lead position when his bomber suffered avionics problems. 60-0060 fired eight CALCMs at targets around Baghdad and completed four missions with 'gravity' bombs during OIF I (as marked on the scoreboard stencilled onto the aircraft's forward fuselage), although it is seen here armed with LGBs shortly after the fighting had ended (*USAF*)

Occasionally, all three types would launch together in a single strike package to attack several targets simultaneously. This was the case in one of the attacks on Baghdad during the first ten days of OIF I, with B-1Bs from the 405th AEW (Provisional) rendezvousing with US-based B-2As and B-52Hs of the 40th AEW (comprising aircraft from all four combat-coded B-52H squadrons) to make simultaneous attacks on enemy command and control centres.

## THE OPPOSITION

On the eve of *Desert Storm*, the IrAF was the world's sixth largest air force, with more than 1000 aircraft. Iraq also possessed 19,000 SAMs and 10,000 AAA pieces, which were all part of an Integrated Air Defence System (IADS) that featured a comprehensive radar network. Attrition during *Desert Storm* and subsequent skirmishes reduced the Iraqi arsenal to around 400 SAMs at 60 sites and 6000 AAA pieces, while the IrAF's 300 remaining fighters (including some that had returned from Iran, where they had fled during *Desert Storm*) were, in many cases, unserviceable or hidden in storage sites.

On the eve of OIF I, the Central Intelligence Agency had established that the IrAF was virtually dysfunctional, with low morale and widespread unairworthiness amongst its surviving aircraft. It was clear that large bombers like the B-52H were at low risk of fighter interception, and in fact no IrAF jets attempted to engage Coalition aircraft during OIF I, allegedly on Saddam Hussein's orders.

The Iraqi IADS network had also been significantly reduced by direct air attacks on any sites that were detected during Operation *Southern Focus* from June 2002. The SAM threat to US aircraft was still important, however. More than 100 had been fired at Coalition aircraft, including a U-2R, between 16 February and 9 May 2001 alone. Fifteen of these 'Dragon Lady' reconnaissance aircraft were subsequently used during the campaign, often with three orbiting over Iraq simultaneously during eight-hour missions. NFZ incursions by surviving Mach 2.4-capable MiG-25 interceptors also increased immediately prior to OIF I.

Baghdad was still surrounded by a 'Super MEZ' (missile engagement zone) that had not been attacked since *Desert Storm*, and Iraq's complex IADS was thought by some planners to require 14 days of attrition by air before a land campaign could start. The capital had a multi-layered missile defence barrier, with radar operators who had been advised by Serb IADS specialists with experience gained during OAF. Initial target lists, assembled from February 2002 by US and British planners, included 300 IADS facilities and 350 airfields among a total of 1000 target aim points per day.

Other estimates by Gen Franks foresaw 45 days to deploy forces and another 45 days of air operations before boots hit the ground. Eventually, a shorter timescale was established with roughly concurrent air and ground operations, and 4000 highly detailed target folders were prepared before hostilities began.

Work on the folders had commenced in October 2002, involving USAF experts on the CALCMs carried by the B-52H and the combat potential of the B-2A. Although Stratofortresses and Lancers could operate from Fairford, the $60 m project to provide operational facilities for the Spirit at the base was not yet completed. Instead, the movement of specially adapted maintenance shelters to Diego Garcia was announced ahead of the B-2A deployment.

The B-52Hs' cruise missiles were to be launched against pre-planned targets during the first few days of the operation. Thereafter, they could be used against targets that required a quick, unplanned attack. Other staff worked on the complex logistics for a massive air operation, including basic requirements like fuel. Fortunately, Saudi Arabia agreed to allow its Prince Sultan Air Base to be used, with aircraft fuelled by thousands of trucks. Just deploying 180 aircraft to their forward bases took 1696 tanker sorties and 245 million pounds of fuel.

The planners also arranged for 3000 PGMs and cruise missiles to be available for the first 48 hours of air strikes – far more than were used in *Desert Storm*. Neighbouring countries provided the Coalition with 27 air bases. Diego Garcia's B-52H detachment had remained in place since OEF, with additional crews and aircraft from the 2nd BW's 20th and 96th BSs increasing the number of bombers assigned to the 40th AEW (commanded by Col Floyd Carpenter) to 14 from March 2003.

A further 14 B-52Hs from Minot were to be based at Fairford with the 16th Air Expeditionary Task Force. They came from the 23rd BS, supplemented by 917th Wing AFRC personnel. The airfield had received a $100 m upgrade in 2000–02, funded mainly by NATO, with US contributions, in its largest infrastructure project since the Cold War. Politically, UN support for a war was prevented by the promise of a French veto, and Turkey's withdrawal of permission to use its airspace and its bases at the last moment prevented important elements of the US Navy and USAF plans from being implemented. The overflight ban was rescinded for the third day of operations, but the crucial Turkish bases remained unavailable.

To preserve the worldwide bomber presence at this difficult time, 12 B-52Hs were also sent to Andersen AFB for the 7th AEW, which used them to monitor potential Chinese or North Korean activity.

The first of 14 B-52Hs from the 23rd BS at Minot began to arrive at Fairford for the 457th AEG on 3 March, whereupon they began two weeks of training missions against a political background of huge 'Stop the War' demonstrations and attempted base invasions by anti-war protestors. The bombers' refuelling requirements were met by an ANG force of 18 KC-135s from Kansas, Tennessee and Pennsylvania based at Mildenhall, with forward-based tankers flying out of RAF Akrotiri, in Cyprus, Souda Bay, on Crete, and Bourgas, in Bulgaria.

The main air offensive began on 20 March (28 hours after major land advances had commenced) with attacks on a reduced number of targets in Baghdad, as it was hoped that Saddam's regime would quickly collapse and his Republican Guard 'shield' might be persuaded to surrender in the face of vastly superior forces. Even so, 1700 bombing sorties were flown against 1000 targets on 20–21 March, together with 504 cruise missile attacks and an initial strike on Baghdad by F-117As. Ten B-52Hs with 96th BS crews released 76 CALCMs at military targets in the Baghdad area – the largest such attack by Stratofortresses to date. The Diego Garcia-based aircraft expended updated AGM-86C Block 1A and AGM-86D Block 2 CALCMs, marking the revised weapon's combat debut, together with JDAM.

Baghdad was also the target for 70 US Navy aircraft flying from three carriers in the Northern Arabian Gulf, and its vital communications tower was hit by two 4700-lb GBU-37 penetrators from one of five B-2A Spirits. The SEAD effort intensified with numerous night attacks by B-2As, F-117As and CALCM-launching B-52Hs, while F-16CJs tried to persuade IADS radar operators to switch their sets on so that they could be hit by HARM. Storm Shadow missiles fired by RAF Tornado GR 4s also obliterated several military command targets in the city. The first attack by eight bomb-armed B-52Hs from Fairford was launched on the morning of 21 March, each aircraft carrying 12 GBU-31s internally. By 2 April they were also hauling 16 CBU-105 WCMDs.

A massive sandstorm shortly after OIF I commenced threatened to hold up the US Army's advance on Baghdad, and it grounded most of the tactical aircraft that were supporting this rapid thrust. Undeterred, the B-52H and B-1B units, flying above the storms, used the detection power of E-8C Joint Surveillance Target Attack Radar System (Joint STARS) aircraft to identify Iraqi armour and artillery positions as targets for their JDAM and WCMDs.

All strikes, including those by the 'stealth' bombers, had jamming support from EA-6B Prowlers. The stealthy aircraft fitted easily into strike packages. When the defences were sufficiently degraded, non-stealthy aircraft were allowed into the 'Super MEZ'. In fact, as Col Carpenter noted, 'We flew directly overhead downtown Baghdad on the second night'.

The first mission by all three bombers took place on 29 March. Launching from separate bases, they jointly attacked command and control centres in Baghdad with PGMs. Iraq's air defences now consisted of SAMs and AAA only, for the IrAF's surviving aircraft had been stood down. Although the SAM inventory had been depleted during *Desert Storm* and Operation *Southern Watch/Southern Strike*, there were still about 1000 MANPADS of various types and 400 longer-ranging SA-2, SA-3, SA-6, SA-8 and Roland SAMs on strength.

40th AEW B-52H 60-0015, which had also seen action in *Desert Fox*, delivered its load of JDAM and Mk 82 bombs on Republican Guard positions and an ammunition storage facility, both within the heavily defended 'Super MEZ' area around Baghdad, on 30 March. Unusually, SEAD support for the mission was unavailable, leaving the crew to rely on their own electronic countermeasures, deft manoeuvring and inaccurate Iraqi firing to defeat several SA-3s and heavy AAA. The B-52H had lost one engine during its inbound flight, and a second engine in the same nacelle gave up on the return leg, but the crew returned to Diego Garcia safely after the 16-hour mission.

As in OEF, multiple targeting became common. On another mission, a 23rd BS crew was requested to hit a Ba'ath Party HQ building and fuel storage tanks near Mosul, followed by Iraqi artillery positions and a WMD plant near Kirkuk and then another fuel storage facility that required a return to the Mosul area. JDAM and M117 bombs were dropped, and when the Stratofortress was targeted by a series of SAMs,

EA-6Bs neutralised the threat by targeting their guidance radar systems with AGM-88 HARM.

After the initial 'Shock and Awe' strikes, the focus shifted to attacks on Iraqi forces in the open, particularly the six Republican Guard divisions around Baghdad. During the entire campaign, most sorties, including those flown by B-52Hs, provided CAS in support of the land war. The constant pounding by heavy bombers with enormous bomb loads caused widespread troop desertions, leaving hundreds of tanks and armoured vehicles abandoned. The psychological impact of a B-52 strike was still the same as it had been in Vietnam more than 30 years earlier.

Tanks in designated 'kill boxes' between Kuwait and Baghdad were targeted by PGMs, and more than 1000 were destroyed before land forces reached Baghdad. In one JDAM attack, 30 T-72 main battle tanks were knocked out. In another, a troop of US Army C Company, 3-7 Cavalry soldiers, surrounded by Iraqi troops in a typical local dust storm, was saved by a B-52H strike that eliminated many of the enemy and enabled 150 Iraqi prisoners to be taken. The US Cavalrymen suffered no casualties in return.

In a relatively short time the Republican Guard units defending Baghdad were neutralised by air strikes, obviating the need for tank-versus-tank battles. USAF bombers continued the attrition of Iraqi armour when the Republican Guard positioned its surviving tanks in covered revetments around the city. Tanks could be geolocated by Joint STARS or drones so that bombers or tactical strikers could be called in. To minimise collateral damage in urban areas, tanks could be hit with 500-lb BDU-50 'concrete' practice bombs fitted with GBU-12 laser guidance kits, the kinetic energy of the weapon being sufficient to disable the target with a direct hit.

As the B-52Hs took on more support missions, the targeting planners had to devise 'bomber boxes' at set coordinates of length, width and magnetic heading in which Stratofortresses could be held to deal with any targets which might emerge.

The wait for a target could be a long one while crew in the AWACS or Joint STARS managing the missions dealt with many other demands, and bombers would sometimes have to refuel in flight during their patrol times. The B-52Hs' long loiter time often allowed these missions to be

23rd BS B-52H-155-BW 60-0051 *APPETITE FOR DESTRUCTION II* returns to a misty Fairford with empty underwing pylons following a 457th AEG-controlled OIF I mission in late March 2003. Four years earlier, the bomber had seen combat during OAF. It later received 'BD' tail codes and the nickname *BELLE STARR* following its transfer from Minot to Barksdale for service with the 93rd BS (*USAF/T Panopalis Archives*)

covered by a single aircraft tackling several 'flex' targets as required, using tactics evolved during OEF. For those missions, their typical loads were 12 JDAM or 16 WCMD canisters on underwing pylons and Mk 82 or Mk 84 GP bombs internally. There were occasional weapons 'hang ups', such as the incident in which B-52H 60-0056 returned safely to Fairford with a hung JDAM on its starboard rack. Several unexpended weapons were also flown back to Fairford at times, or jettisoned near Lundy Island, off the coast of North Devon, in a designated sea area.

B-52Hs of the 457th AEG were an essential part of the Allied offensive in northern Iraq, where Turkish opposition prevented US troops from entering the area from Turkey. This meant that American SOF had to be emplaced in the area to work with Kurdish fighters against Iraqi forces. They used similar CAS tactics to those of OEF in guiding precision air strikes onto Iraqi troop positions. The B-52Hs orbited over potential target areas, requiring frequent air refuelling sessions, ready to deliver JDAM immediately when they received target coordinates from the ground. These missions often lasted up to 15 hours.

## COMBAT HARDWARE

For OIF I, new and more effective weapons became available. Notably, the GPS-aided innovations were relatively unaffected by the lack of clear weather. For the B-52H, one of the most important additions was the AN/AAQ-28(V)3 Litening II targeting pod, later upgraded to AN/AAQ-28(V)4 AT. Available from 2001, but more commonly used by tactical fighter-bombers like the F-16, it conferred greatly increased accuracy, particularly for the night missions usually flown by the Stratofortresses. Although 12 B-52Hs were undergoing conversion to allow them to use the Litening pod after Operational Utility Evaluation was completed in March 2003 in Project *Seek Eagle*, only two were available for OIF I.

Effective with LGBs, GPS-guided ordnance or conventional bombs, Litening includes a FLIR sensor and a CCD-TV camera to gain target imagery from altitudes as high as 35,000 ft for combat identification. This was the sort of altitude from which B-52H and B-1B crews showed that CAS could be provided in OIF I. US Army generals had assumed from past experience that such support missions had to be flown at very low altitudes in order to confront targets precisely.

Combined with the sophisticated sensors and satellite communications systems in the E-8C Joint STARS, the B-52H could also be used against large-scale targets of opportunity. The effectiveness of this partnership was shown during the large sandstorms that enveloped Iraq in the early stages of OIF I. Attempting to take advantage of the adverse weather conditions, which it hoped would disguise its progress, a Republican Guard tank regiment headed south to defend Baghdad. Joint STARS found it and directed B-52Hs in to pulverise the column.

On 11 April a 93rd BS B-52H, crewed by both 23rd and 93rd BS personnel, made the first combat delivery of self-designated LGB from a Stratofortress. Using a Litening II pod, it successfully guided a pair of 500-lb GBU-12 Paveway II LGBs onto two air defence radar targets on Al Sahra airfield.

The PGMs used in *Desert Storm* in 1991 had achieved many spectacular results, but they were then in short supply and comprised only seven per cent of the weapons dropped by tactical aircraft and bombers. They were also limited by poor weather, smoke and dust clouds. For OIF I, that proportion rose to 70 to 80 per cent, even though total numbers were not significantly greater. To a marked extent, this was due to the availability of JDAM – a weapon developed post-1991 in an attempt to remedy the weather and visibility problems associated with LGBs.

During OIF I, the planning staff assessing BDA after missions tended to assume that a correctly delivered JDAM would certainly have hit its target. They only required photographic or other evidence of a hit in the case of particularly high-value targets. The relaxing of the BDA rules reflected the difficulty in keeping up with the damage caused by the vast tonnage of ordnance being dropped by heavy bombers and other aircraft.

JDAM take position data from four or more satellites, and it is vital that those 'heavenly bodies' are themselves in their exact orbits and precisely timed, orbiting at a set distance from each other. Any disparities would result in an inaccurate bomb. Before OIF I, Gen John Jumper, USAF Chief of Staff, expressed concern that Iraq might be able to jam the global GPS satellite system on which JDAM depended. The country had indeed been supplied with Russian GPS jammers in 2003, but they were not used effectively.

The MILSTAR satellite network that US forces relied on had other benefits aside from JDAM targeting. A B-52H crew took off from Fairford but had radio failure soon afterwards. Rather than abandoning the mission, they were able to use MILSTAR and other communications support from the US space programme net to complete their OIF I sortie.

B-52Hs delivered more PGMs than fighter-bombers did, despite the latter being present in considerably greater numbers. Both it and the B-1B reinforced the lasting value of long loiter times near targets, heavy and varied weapons loadouts and long range. A reduction in tanking requirements compared with numerous smaller aircraft was also welcomed. The B-52H's extended loiter times were a long-established part of its Cold War legacy when *Chrome Dome* bombers patrolled for many hours over the Arctic wastes, ready to enter hostile airspace with nuclear weapons at short notice.

The 'heavies' were seen as the real 'workhorses' in the Afghan and Iraq campaigns, both in terms of the proportion of the total delivery of ordnance that they achieved and due to their flexibility and endurance. Already 41 years old when OIF I commenced, the deployed B-52Hs of the 457th AEG were well supplied with $81 m of spare parts to maintain their high rates of availability.

Another innovative weapon introduced for OIF I was the CBU-105 WCMD, a cluster bomb with a Lockheed Martin tail kit that enabled precision delivery, compensating for wind. The kit turned a CBU-86 (CBU-103) combined effects munition, a CBU-97 (CGU-104) sensor-fused weapon or a GBU-98 (CBU-105) GATOR CBU into a PGM. Fairford-based B-52Hs carried 16 on their external pylons for several missions.

Cruising over the vastness of the Indian Ocean, heading north from Diego Garcia to Iraq, this 40th AEW B-52H is laden down with GBU-31 JDAM for a CAS mission in early April 2003. Such sorties typically lasted 16 hours from take-off to recovery (*USAF/T Panopalis Archives*)

Prodigious quantities of ordnance had been delivered by the Fairford-based bombers by the time their task was completed on 1 May. Although B-52H missions from both Diego Garcia and Fairford were scheduled in the final week of April, there were very few targets left. In 120 missions, the 5th BW crews logged 1600 hours. The 20th BS score included 212,000 lbs of JDAM, aimed at Iraqi targets around Baghdad. Overall, the B-52Hs dropped 3.2 million pounds, consisting of 2700 weapons (80 per cent of them PGMs) and nine million propaganda leaflets, flying half of the USAF's heavy bomber missions during the operation.

Use of Fairford-based B-52Hs, together with carrier-based aircraft in the eastern Mediterranean, enabled strikes to be carried out in northern Iraq which were beyond the practical range of land-based aircraft, including RAF Tornado GR IVs based in Kuwait and Qatar, particularly when bad weather or dust storms closed their bases. However, by 4 April, resistance in Iraq was crumbling, and five days later ground forces entered Baghdad and Saddam Hussein's control ended. At this point the B-52Hs shifted their patrols to Tikrit and Mosul in the north of the country, and on 14 April, air operations effectively came to an end for the Stratofortresses.

## OPERATION *INHERENT RESOLVE*

American forces left Iraq in 2011 after eight years, at the official end of the Iraq War. However, by August 2014, Islamic State (IS), now an insurgent army continuing the al-Qaeda cause and led by Abu Bakr al-Baghdadi, was advancing into Iraq after their military successes in Syria, determined to destroy the nation's fragile stability following the cessation of OIF. IS forces were intent on taking the cities of Erbil and Mosul and possibly moving against Baghdad. Their expansion continued until 2019, when a coalition of countries brought an end to the 'caliphate' imposed upon large areas of Iraq and Syria.

USAF air strikes on IS positions commenced on 9 August 2014, and continued for three weeks in what became codenamed Operation *Inherent Resolve*. Its purpose was to destroy IS camps in Syria and northern Iraq and prevent the organisation from growing, attracting foreign recruits to perform terrorist acts abroad. Nevertheless, IS continued to take provincial capitals throughout Iraq, and the American-trained and equipped Iraqi Army seemed unable, or unwilling, to stop them.

As President Obama observed in May 2015, America was in danger of entering another Vietnam situation, backing a regime which seemed incapable of defending itself. By November 2015, Turkey had agreed to allow USAF F-15As, F-15Es, A-10As and drones to operate from Incirlik AB, greatly increasing the range of aerial options against IS. Direct IS threats against the US prompted a B-1B attack on 11 bridges around Raqqa, the IS capital in Syria, on 4 July. By February 2016 US aircraft were hitting up to 15 IS-related targets in a single day.

From 9 April 2016, B-52Hs of the 2nd BW (mainly drawn from the unit's 20th BS), operating with the 380th AEW, relieved the Lancers in the fight to stop IS. The first attack undertaken by a Stratofortress in *Inherent Resolve* took place on 20 April, when a weapons cache was targeted near Qayyarah – this was the first time B-52Hs had dropped ordnance in anger since April 2003. After improvements to the infrastructure at Al Udeid, the aircraft were able to double their strike rate against IS targets to 130 sorties in July, delivering GBU-12 Paveway II LGBs and GBU-31 or GBU-38 JDAM, with eight of the latter mounted on a HSAB on each wing. An alternative 'dumb' bomb load consisted of up to 45 500-lb Mk 82s. Simplifying the process for target approval also facilitated strikes on elusive IS forces.

With increasing Iranian involvement and a lack of tribal fighters willing to resist IS, the American dilemma deepened. It became clear that air power would be the crucial factor, with US advisors working with Iraqi troops and the very few American soldiers directly involved, although *Inherent Resolve* was led by a US Army general. Returning significant US ground forces to the area was unthinkable, but President Obama was also afraid that, 'We can't just win the fight from the air'. However, the aerial campaign proceeded, with participation by units flying B-52Hs and fighter-bombers. Obama's policy, continued by President Trump, was to remove the IS leaders and fight through proxy forces, including the Kurds, supported by copious air power resources. It was also accepted that a limited number of US troops, set at 5000, would have to remain in the area.

Anticipating the re-taking of the city of Fallujah on 29 June 2016, the IS occupation force assembled a large convoy to make their escape. Al Udeid-based B-52Hs cratered the road ahead of the vehicles with JDAM at night, and then, having checked that there were no civilian refugees,

Barksdale B-52Hs 60-0032 from the 96th BS and 60-0025 from the 20th BS arrive at Al Udeid on 6 April 2016 to replace B-1Bs in the fight against IS. A second pair began the journey on 10 April but had to return to Barksdale as there were insufficient tankers to see them to their destination. The 2016 deployment was the first time B-52Hs had been based in Qatar in support of CENTCOM, overall manager of conventional forces assigned to *Inherent Resolve* (*USAF*)

bombed the vehicles, destroying 213 of them. One of the Stratofortresses had been diverted from another mission, where it was meant to cover a Jaysh Maghawir al-Thawra commando force attempting to stem IS advances in Syria. Sadly, the bomber's absence allowed the commando group to be driven back when on the verge of victory.

As the re-taking of Mosul approached, B-52Hs were prominent in a 'quick reaction team' of aircraft relieving Peshmerga fighters near the city on 3 May 2017. IS truck bombs and armoured vehicles were targeted as they tried to cover the thousands of IS warriors in Mosul. Having lost areas around Mosul, the terrorists focused on holding Kirkuk, where they burned down a sulphur factory, releasing clouds of toxic gas towards the recently recaptured Al Qayyarah air base, near Mosul. The USAF had previously used B-52Hs and fighter-bombers to destroy another pharmaceutical plant to prevent IS from using it to make chemical weapons.

The recapture of Mosul was a long and bloody affair. Many CAS missions were flown, including one by B-52Hs called in to drop JDAM on partially collapsed buildings in the old city, whose cellars were refuges for the last groups of IS troops. JDAM cracked open concrete floors so that further bombs could penetrate the basements. US bombing continued until 9 July, and the city was liberated the following day.

In September of the previous year, the 96th EBS had taken over the B-52H mission at Al Udeid in September 2016, bringing with it the Combat Network Communication Technology (CONECT) system and the 500-lb GBU-54 Laser JDAM. Both innovations facilitated targeting and accuracy. The squadron had flown 729 sorties by 20 February 2017, when it was replaced by the 23rd EBS, making its first combat deployment for 12 years.

Missions against IS from Al Udeid fell into two categories – 'deliberate' strikes against pre-planned key targets in the enemy's rear area (such as the bridges around Raqqa, the Syrian centre of IS power, by B-1Bs) and 'dynamic' attacks against troops in contact with Iraqi and Kurdish troops. By mid-2015, the vast majority were 'dynamic'.

As previously noted, an example of the latter occurred on 29 June 2016 when a large convoy of IS vehicles was detected apparently advancing from Fallujah on the sacred Shiite city of Karbala. B-52Hs with JDAM, were

A B-52H of the 23rd EBS taxis out at Al Udeid at the start of an *Inherent Resolve* mission in June 2017. The aircraft is armed with both 500-lb GBU-54 and 2000-lb GBU-31 JDAM. Note how close the bomber's outrigger wheels are to the edges of the taxiway, the latter having been widened in early 2016 specifically to allow B-52Hs to operate from Al Udeid (*USAF*)

called in from Al Udeid to crater the road and halt the convoy. When it was established that the vehicles contained armed personnel only, 213 of them were destroyed or damaged. One of the Stratofortresses involved in the attack had been diverted from its planned mission supporting US-backed fighters in northern Syria. Fortunately, a Predator UAV was also in the area to take out an IS suicide bomb truck which could have hit the fighters in the B-52H's absence.

Flying over conspicuously inhospitable terrain, a B-52H disconnects from a KC-135R tanker in July 2017. Its combat load includes 2000- and 500-lb JDAM and a targeting pod, the latter located under the right wing (*USAF/T Panopalis Archives*)

Stratofortresses were also involved in 'quick reaction team' air strikes as Iraqi troops advanced on Mosul to recapture the city. Their missions were effectively CAS for troops in contact, working with A-10As and fighter-bombers. In a large-scale operation by Kurdish, Peshmerga and Iraqi forces, with US Marine Corps advisors, Coalition air forces were hard pressed to meet the demands for CAS.

In another strike near Mosul on 12 September 2016, B-52Hs and tactical aircraft bombed a large pharmaceutical complex which was thought to be producing chlorine and mustard gas for IS. Although the recapture of Mosul was a gruelling house-by-house infantry operation that took nine months to complete, precision air strikes, often with JDAM, took out specific IS targets on many occasions, allowing Coalition troops to move forward. In one attack, a 0.50-cal machine gun positioned above a hospital was cleared by a single bomb, saving many Coalition lives.

The last stand by IS in Mosul took place in a ruined urban area of the Old City where the fighters were sheltering in the basements of collapsed buildings. B-52Hs dropped JDAM to fracture the concrete above the cellars to enable other weapons to penetrate down into the interiors. This tactic was often frustrated by IS using civilian human shields, and after 16 July 2017, bombing was ruled out as the remaining IS members were in such close quarters to the Iraqi Army.

The B-52H detachment was involved in supporting US troops and the Syrian Democratic Forces (SDF) after the latter stormed the IS 'capital', Raqqa, in June 2017 in an operation which the US code-named *Eclipse*. It involved moving F-15Es to airfields in Jordan to reduce range requirements. F-22A Raptors were also on hand, as Russia had based numerous fighters in Syria in support of President Bashar al-Assad.

After allowing more than 2000 IS insurgents to evacuate the city, the SDF then planned to move south and secure oil and gas fields. Assad's Russian-backed forces also moved towards the oilfields, and a tense confrontation ensued in which Russian Wagner Group mercenary troops fired artillery rounds at the relatively small number of US troops across an unofficial dividing line between Russian and US-controlled positions. When the Wagner Group assault developed into an armoured advance on

GBU-54 JDAM have been attached to the inner underwing pylon of a 69th EBS B-52H in October 2017, this ordnance subsequently being used against IS in northern Iraq (*USAF*)

the Americans, their tanks and artillery were hit by B-52Hs, F-15Es and helicopter gunships until the Russian-speaking force, which had sought to take over the local oilfield, turned back. The group's motive, at Russia's behest, although the connection was denied in Moscow, had been to profit from the oil reserves. Shortly thereafter, President Trump lost interest in Syria.

Nevertheless, improvements to the B-52H continued to reach frontline units. Amongst them was the CRL – a modification of the CSRL that became operational in Barksdale Stratofortresses on 19 November 2017 as part of the Mil Std 1760 Internal Weapons Bay Upgrade. CRL made its B-52H combat debut with a 69th EBS aircraft during a February 2018 *Jagged Knife* mission to Afghanistan towards the end of the 2nd BW's Al Udeid stay. Six CRLs had originally been delivered to the 2nd BW in 2016, providing a 60 per cent increase in the payload of 'dumb bombs' and 'smart' weapons including JDAM and JASSM, which previously could only be carried on the wing pylons. The *Jagged Knife* mission also set a record for the highest number of PGMs delivered during a single B-52H sortie.

In an operation against Taliban positions and vehicles in Tajikistan, 24 PGMs were dropped – up to 30 could be carried, including an additional eight internally, which meant that, theoretically, 30 separate targets could be destroyed in one sortie. Some of the vehicles targeted in Tajikistan were stolen Afghan National Army trucks that were being converted into truck bombs. *Jagged Knife* was intended to disrupt the Taliban's vital and resurgent drug industry. It occupied an increasing number of B-52H missions in 2018 as the requirement for *Inherent Resolve* missions declined.

Prior to that, during operations against IS in 2017, B-52Hs achieved a record number of 834 CENTCOM missions with no maintenance cancellations. Overall, in two years of flying from Al Udeid, the Stratofortresses completed 1850 sorties and delivered 12,000 weapons. In the first phase of the deployment, using B-52Hs from the 23rd BS (which celebrated its 100th anniversary in June 2017), 400 consecutive sorties were flown with no maintenance cancellations, and the 69th BS contingent subsequently took that total to 834 when it rotated in.

Amongst the sorties flown by the latter squadron were strike missions into eastern Syria during the Battle of Khasham on 7 February 2018.

Based at Al Udeid from April 2016, the B-52Hs finally returned to the USA, via the Pacific, in June 2018 when upgraded 34th EBS B-1Bs took over the *Inherent Resolve* tasking for supporting operations in Afghanistan, Syria and Iraq. Mission totals (for the Stratofortress and the Lancer) exceeded previous records set by B-52D/G units during Operation *Linebacker II* in 1972.

When the Stratofortresses finally withdrew from Al Udeid in April 2018 for further operations in the Pacific area, 69th EBS commander Lt Col Paul Goossen commented that the bomber was 'such a versatile airframe that it keeps being reinvented and keeps showing its usefulness and its relevance in every war that America finds itself in. Every day in support of partner and Coalition ground forces, our B-52s delivered on-call, ready firepower and intelligence, surveillance and reconnaissance [ISR] capability. We maintained a 24/7 presence over the battlefield hunting IS and Taliban targets. Through our continuous ISR and precision strikes in support of the Iraqi Security Forces and SDFs' ground scheme of manoeuvre, we helped contribute to the liberation of more than 7.7 million people and approximately 98 per cent of territory formerly controlled by IS'.

B-52Hs from the 23rd BS at Minot were detached to Al Udeid once again in April 2020 for a six-month deployment as the withdrawal of US troops from Afghanistan gathered pace. They completed 3100 hours of combat flying totalling 240 sorties. Four replacement Minot aircraft arrived to maintain the coverage from 23 April 2021. *Inherent Resolve* continued into the next US presidency, with 50 air strikes against IS targets occurring in the first seven months of President Biden's tenure. The operation eventually ended the IS caliphate, which, at its height, had covered 41,000 square miles and controlled eight million people. A large Coalition force had eliminated many of the 65,000 adherents to the movement, including several leaders, in more than 33,000 air and artillery strikes. The vast majority of strikes were undertaken by US aircraft, with RAF fighter-bombers contributing the second highest number. *Inherent Resolve* remains an active operation in Iraq, Syria and Libya, despite the widespread defeat of IS.

69th EBS munitions technicians load JDAM onto a CRL within the bomb-bay of a B-52H at Al Udeid in November 2017. The CRL subsequently made its combat debut with the 69th during a February 2018 *Jagged Knife* mission to Afghanistan (*USAF*)

Aircrew from the 69th EBS crowd around B-52H-165-BW 61-0013 *HIGH TENSION III* (complete with a detailed bomb log) on the ramp at Al Udeid shortly after the bomber had completed the unit's last mission of the deployment prior to turning the *Inherent Resolve* mission tasking over to B-1Bs of the 34th EBS. Since the B-52H's arrival in-theatre in April 2016, the aircraft had flown more than 1800 operational sorties and dropped almost 12,000 weapons on IS and Taliban targets (*USAF*)

## CHAPTER SIX

# READY FOR THE FUTURE

69th EBS B-52H-150-BW 60-0037 *WHAM BAM II* shares the Andersen AFB flightline with a pair of 23rd EBS aircraft, also from Minot AFB, on 12 July 2019. This much-travelled Stratofortress, previously nicknamed *Black Widow*, also flew many OAF missions in 1999 and, 22 years later, participated in the final stages of OEF (*USAF/T Panopalis Archives*)

Having provided a credible nuclear deterrent from English airfields for decades, the Stratofortress continued to be on call as the 'big stick', returning there at times of international tension. Regular deployments to Britain for NATO exercises have long been seen as a means of demonstrating that deterrent presence. B-52Hs first deployed to Fairford for NATO Exercise *Central Enterprise* on 19–29 June 1993. At that time, the five aircraft (61-0003, 61-0008, 61-0017, 61-0028 and 61-0040) belonged to the 92nd BW at Fairchild AFB, Washington, and wore the unit's 'seahawk' motif on their tails.

Exercise *Bright Star*, resuming in November 1993 after an eight-year hiatus, took B-52Hs from the 2nd, 5th, 410th and 419th BWs to Egypt to maintain the Atlantic 'Bomber Bridge'. Longer transpacific sorties taking up to 25 hours by B-52Hs developed the Global Power concept that promised the presence of bombers at short notice wherever they were required. Exercise *Northern Viking* in July 1995 included a pair of Minot's B-52Hs for the first time. Flying from Keflavik, Iceland, where perimeter lights had to be removed from some sections of the taxiways to accommodate the bombers' wide outrigger landing gears, they flew at very low altitude, simulating Russian bomber strikes on the airfield, to provide the locally-based F-15C Eagle pilots with interception practice.

The 23rd BS and other 2nd BW units routinely deployed to Guam, a regular temporary home for B-52s since the 1960s, from March

2004 until 2016 as part of US Pacific Command's policy of keeping a Continuous Bomber Presence (CBP) in the Pacific region. In February 2004 five of Minot AFB's B-52Hs arrived at Andersen AFB. The USAF stated that they would stay for 'an undetermined period in support of US Pacific Command', and ACC maintained that commitment with a series of B-52H rotations as required.

The 5th BW used its 2016 deployment to Guam to fly B-52H 60-0055, with a Republic of Korea Air Force F-15K and F-16C escort over South Korea at low-altitude after North Korean thermonuclear bomb tests. This 'big stick' flight was intended to 'demonstrate the ironclad US commitment to our allies in South Korea, in Japan and to the defence of the American homeland', according to Adm Harry B Harris, Commander, US Pacific Command. In March 2013, B-52Hs had dropped weapons on the Pil-sung Range near Osan, in South Korea, simulating attacks further north, during Exercise *Foal Eagle*. The CBP concept was replaced by the Bomber Task Force (BTF) in 2023, increasing flexibility and 'operational unpredictability'.

In January 2018, six 2nd BW B-52Hs returned to Guam, where they joined three B-2As and six B-1Bs from the 37th EBS, the latter aircraft subsequently departing to Ellsworth AFB shortly thereafter following six months on the island. Whilst there, they participated in annual *Cope North* exercises with aircraft from six other Pacific region countries. CBP deployments lasted for six months, and usually required six Stratofortresses and 300 personnel.

The B-52H's global reach was demonstrated in a 1 July 2015 non-stop flight from Barksdale to deliver inert bombs on the Delamere Air Weapons Range in Australia's Northern Territory. The aircraft that undertook the mission, B-52H 61-0015, had previously appeared at the Australian International Airshow at Avalon Airport, Victoria, some five months earlier. In March 2019 the 23rd BS returned to Australia when two B-52Hs were sent to Royal Australian Air Force (RAAF) Base Darwin, in the Northern Territory, for Exercise *Diamond Shield*. B-52H detachments are likely to be based at Tindal, also in the Northern Territory, in response to increased tension caused by China's military expansion in the South China Sea area. Additional fuel tanks, weapons storage space and support facilities for up to six B-52s are planned for the base by 2026.

*Talisman Sabre* exercises were held from the summer of 2021 using 23rd BS aircraft to test interoperability with Australian forces. Basing B-52s in the Northern Territory compensates to some extent for the lack of B-52-capable runways in Southeast Asia in the event of Taiwan requiring further US military support. Also, both Guam and Japan are within range of several types of Chinese surface-to-surface missiles.

Within NATO's sphere of influence, the 2nd BW sent three B-52Hs to Moron AB, Spain, on 27 February 2016 for Exercise *Cold Response* over central Norway. Long associated with deployments by SAC and AAC bombers and tankers, Moron is a European alternative to Fairford, but with better weather. At the latter base, B-52Hs are frequent visitors, and in August 2016 aircraft stopped over here en route from Sliač, Slovakia, where they had taken part in Exercise *Ample Strike*.

Emphasising the B-52H's continuing role as a deterrent to all other potential aggressors, three aircraft from the 2nd and 5th BWs retraced most of the Cold War *Chrome Dome* polar route on 31 July 2016. Together with two 509th BW B-2As, they crossed the North and Baltic Seas, the North Pole and Alaska, before returning over the Aleutian Islands, in Exercise *Polar Roar*.

Training within the USA includes participation in *Red Flag* exercises and the annual Exercise *Global Thunder*. One of the regular B-52 deployments to England while Afghan operations continued was for Baltic Operations (BALTOPS) 16 and *Saber Strike* in June 2016. These exercises were unusual in focusing on maritime cooperation with NATO warships. The three versatile Minot AFB 23rd BS aircraft with 'Mighty' and 'Icer' callsigns, commanded by Col Keiran Denehan, flew with inert Mk 62 Quick Strike mines, carrying 27 in their bomb-bays and 18 on the wing pylons, which were delivered in set patterns at low-altitude.

The frequent BALTOPs exercises have been held to lend reassurance to Eastern Europe in the light of increasing Russian hostility in Georgia and Ukraine. In June 2017, a BALTOPS brought all three US strategic bombers to Fairford. Three 2nd BW B-52Hs, two B-1Bs from the 28th BW and a pair of 509th BW B-2As flew practice missions over the Baltic Sea, where they were regularly intercepted by Russian Su-27 fighters.

B-52Hs on deployment to Guam also practised Quick Strike mining. *Saber Strike* involved the use of AN/AAQ-33 Sniper pods against ground targets on a range. Sniper began integration trials with a 49th TES B-52H at Barksdale in June 2008, the 419th Flight Test Squadron (FTS) having cleared the pod for the B-1B in February 2007. Sniper had its combat debut with a 34th EBS B-1B in Afghanistan in August 2008. B-52Hs joined the attempts to suppress IS terrorist groups in Operation *Inherent Resolve* over Syria and Iraq in April 2016.

Long-distance flights or 'presence patrols' are a good chance to interact with other air forces en route. 69th EBS B-52H 61-0039 completed a 23 hr 25 min marathon from Fairford to the Middle East on 14 February 2022, meeting up with escorting fighters from the RAF, the US Marine Corps, the Royal Jordanian Air Force, the Egyptian Air Force and the Royal Saudi Air Force en route. Together with 61-0003, 61-0018 and 60-0044 as 'Hate 11-14', it had also attracted company from Portuguese Air Force F-16AMs and RAF Typhoons in crossing over Iceland on the way to a simulated range-drop of JDAM, before arriving for a three-week sojourn at Fairford in response to Soviet military activity on the border with Ukraine.

Earlier, in August–September 2020, pairs of 5th BW aircraft, with escorts from numerous NATO partners, flew a series of *Allied Sky* training flights to assert freedom of navigation and overflight rights across the Black Sea. They attracted the attention of Russian fighters from Crimea, which intercepted two B-52Hs on 28 August. The bomber crews practised cruise missile launches within 18 miles of the Russian border. Training missions from Fairford in October 2022 included Minot B-52Hs as the focus of packages with Swedish Air Force JAS 39 Gripen fighters and F-16Cs of the Turkish Air Force.

Routine BTF-Europe deployments continued in 2024, including a visit by four 69th BS B-52Hs from Minot in May. Their missions included participation in Exercise *African Lion* over Morocco, working with 27 other national armed forces. US strategic bombers visited Romania for the first time on 21 July 2024 when two Barksdale B-52Hs operated out of the country for BTF 24-4. They were intercepted by Russian aircraft over the Barents Sea, but 'did not change their course' and were able to 'perform their pre-planned mission, which included integration alongside NATO fighter aircraft', according to a USAFE-AFAFRICA statement.

## BETTER 'BUFFs'

The progressive addition of advanced stand-off weapons to the B-52H's inventory has maintained its credibility as a long-range striker in the age of the stealthy B-2A and B-21 bombers. Given effective SEAD, it will also remain an invaluable 'bomb truck' over any potential target. *Desert Storm* saw the concept of integrated force deployments beginning to involve B-52s, whereas previously units had managed their own overseas deployments under strict SAC supervision. The bombers began to operate far more closely with E-3 Sentry, RC-135 *Rivet Joint* and Joint STARS reconnaissance and control platforms to identify and hit their targets.

Improvements to the B-52H have continued throughout its long life. The USAF's $11.9 bn sustainment programme was launched on 12 October 2010, at a cost of more than $150 m per Stratofortress. B-52Hs were seen as a good long-term investment, with better mission-capable rates than the B-1B (75.8 per cent against 61.2 per cent in 2007, although this rate has varied since). In 2019, the Bomber Vector programme was designed to equip 75 B-52Hs for service after the withdrawal of the B-1B and B-2A.

The January 2000 Offensive Avionics System upgrades combined with more advanced communications systems in the form of a CONECT system, developed and installed from 2009 to 2020, all help to integrate the B-52H more effectively within modern combat scenarios. It was first used during Operation *Inherent Resolve*. CONECT incorporates a Bomber Tactical Data Link (Link 16) which gives the veteran B-52H jam-resistant command and control communications that enables it to conduct missions in high-threat environments. Full-colour multi-function displays, real-time data displayed on moving maps and advanced computers greatly increase the bomber's integration into a comprehensive, hi-tech communications network and allow it to revise its mission parameters or re-target weapons instantly during a sortie.

The first CONECT B-52H was delivered in May 2014. Tests of an extremely high frequency satellite communications system began in 2009 as part of the improved connections capability, with sources on the ground, in the air and in space.

Until 2001, the aircraft's AN/ALT-28 electronic countermeasures (ECM) equipment had not been significantly upgraded since the mid-1960s apart from the addition of receiver and sensor capabilities, which redesignated the suite as the AN/ALQ-155. Radar warning receiver updates in Project *Pave Mint*, including the AN/ALR-46 digital system, greatly increased the B-52H's survivability, and later improvements to the AN/ALQ-172 ECM suite after OAF broadened the range of air defence threats to which it could respond.

In the closing stages of OAF, the possibility of fielding an ECM version of the B-52H was considered as a supplement to the overworked EA-6B Prowler. One aircraft was modified to take the Prowler's AN/ALQ-99 jamming pod, but the EA-18G Growler was chosen as a replacement instead. To a greater extent than its more advanced Cold War contemporary bombers, the B-52H requires air superiority and ECM support to be assured of its safety over likely target areas for any attacks other than those with long-range stand-off weapons. In the majority of the operations it has undertaken since 1993, that has been the case.

By 2026 the Radar Modernization Program will provide a new wide-band radome containing a phased array replacement for the 'legacy' AN/APQ-166 mechanically-scanned radar, as well as new radar control touchscreens, hand controllers and sensor processors for the radar navigators to use. First requested in 2014 as the Strategic Radar Replacement, the improved radar will have an electronically-scanned array, moving target tracking and electronic protection.

The AN/ASQ-181 electro-optical weapons system was retained, but from late 2003 the external Litening targeting pod, followed by the Sniper AT pod, were more often used. Learning to use the Sniper became one of the most challenging aspects of the 307th BW's training course. Rather than bombing 'blind' above cloud in the traditional way, the crew had to see and study the target with the Sniper and make very sure that it was the correct one as per the coordinates.

From 2003 to 2009, an avionics midlife improvement programme (AMI) was begun for the AN/ASQ-176 offensive avionics system, fitting new inertial navigation and weapons systems, together with increased computer capacity and new radios. AMI allows the crew to operate several Stores Management Overlays simultaneously, each one of which controls a separate weapon, rather than being able to launch only one type at a time. For example, a CALCM could be prepared for launch at the same time as a JASSM, rather than the crew having to effectively re-programme the system between weapons. Two B-52Hs, 60-0036 and 60-0050, were used by the Air Force Flight Test Center (AFFTC) to test the system, which entered service from 2006.

The Lockheed Martin AN/AAQ-33 Sniper AT pod followed the Litening targeting pod into service with the B-52H during the early 2000s, these modestly sized external stores turning the Stratofortress into a precision bomber when armed with JDAM or LGBs (*USAF*)

One of the main criticisms of the B-52H's targeting system during combat operations was its lack of capability against moving targets. Andersen AFB hosted 20th BS B-52Hs (including 60-0061, 60-0053 and 61-0002) and Dyess-based

B-1Bs for Exercise *Resultant Fury* in November 2004 to test Northrop Grumman's Affordable Moving Surface Target Engagement system. It provided GPS-guided weapons with data from a Joint STARS or E-3 Sentry. After a weapon was dropped, that data was supplied to it, updating tracking information until impact in all weathers.

One solution to the moving target issue came with Laser JDAM which adds a DSU-38 precision laser seeker to a 500-lb GBU-38 JDAM, making it a GBU-54. The similar DSU-40 converts a 2000-lb JDAM into a GBU-56, and both incorporate anti-jamming of GPS signals – a major threat to GPS weapons which the Russians have sometimes exploited in Ukraine. The weapons can be updated in flight to follow and destroy moving targets.

In *Resultant Fury*, off Hawaii, B-52Hs hit two large, towed targets moving at 14 knots and three B-52Hs sank the decommissioned 522-ft long tank landing ship USS *Schenectady* (LST-1185) with direct hits by 2000-lb JDAM and a Litening pod-directed GBU-10 LGB. Capt Ronald Wheeler, who operated the Litening pod and managed the GBU-10 delivery, commented, 'To see the LST through the targeting pod I was using to lase the ship, and to see it blow up in real time, was pretty exciting. Any hostile surface vessel should take heed'.

The LGB-launching B-52H from the 49th TES flew for ten hours directly from Barksdale, with aircraft commander Maj Terry Christiansen at the controls. He recalled, 'Since we released all four [LGBs] simultaneously, 8000 lbs of weight came off at the same time. So you feel it. This is the first time a B-52 has gone out and dropped self-designated laser-guided weapons on a moving ship. It's pretty significant'.

Twelve JDAM or 16 WCMD, attached to underwing pylons, together with new wiring and digital buses in ongoing modifications will ensure that both 'dumb' and guided weapons can be carried on the pylons simultaneously. B-52Hs can also carry updated Quick Strike Extended Range mines that can be dropped from safer, higher altitudes than standard Quick Strike models.

In May 2010, 419th FTS B-52H 60-0050 flight-tested the Boeing X-51 Waverider hypersonic vehicle, powered by a booster rocket and

The smouldering hulk of decommissioned tank landing ship *Schenectady* was photographed after it had been hit by several bombs dropped from three B-52Hs during *Resultant Fury* in November 2004. The vessel was subsequently struck by still more ordnance, sending it to the bottom of the Pacific Ocean some distance off Hawaii (*USAF*)

scramjet engine, from Edwards AFB. In a May 2013 launch, the X-51 reached Mach 5.1 for six minutes. The vehicle is intended to enable the development of both hypersonic reconnaissance and missile technology, with an X-51 derivative potentially being carried by a B-52H to give the aircraft a stand-off offensive capability to rival the air-launched AS-24 'Killjoy' ballistic missile used against Ukraine by Russia from 2022.

The Lockheed Martin AGM-183A Air-Launched Rapid Response Weapon (ARRW) 'boost-glide' long-range air-launched hypersonic missile was given a captive-carry flight by the 419th FTS on 12 June 2019, and it reached Mach 5 in its first live launch on 9 December 2022. Although officially cancelled in mid-2023, it could still form the basis of a hypersonic stand-off weapon for the B-52H.

In 2016, the 2nd BW used both Litening and Sniper pods operationally, switching between them as one or the other was being upgraded. The projected B-52J and B-52K will dispense with the chin turrets for Low-Light TV and infra-red targeting systems (which do not provide targeting capability) in favour of external pods and new electronically-scanned Raytheon radar, developed from the AN/APG-79/82 radar used by the F/A-18E/F Super Hornet.

Although most of the B-52H's weapons are currently stand-off types, enemy air defence systems still pose a threat – particularly long-range SAMs. In training sessions such as *Roving Sands*, Stratofortress crews learned how to cope with enemy IADS during joint composite strike missions by employing weapons such as air-launched cruise missiles or JDAM.

With the lack of a manned aerial threat assuring the demise of the bomber's rear gunner immediately after *Desert Storm*, the USAF is presently looking at reducing the flightdeck crew to four – a serious diminution of the numbers required in earlier B-52 models, where at least seven were needed. Current training aims to qualify two crew as pilots and the others on all three crew stations as navigators and electronic warfare operators. Cost-cutters are conscious that the B-1B can be flown by four crew and the B-2A by just two.

The USAF has undoubtedly benefitted financially from the B-52's longevity. It has sometimes been noted that when the first XB-52 was being constructed, the last American Civil War veteran was still alive. Over almost 75 years, its versatility and availability have partly compensated for the unexpectedly small size of the B-2A fleet, and although it has required frequent updates to its avionics and weapons, the Stratofortress has needed far fewer maintenance hours and cost appreciably less than its intended successors.

Furthermore, unlike the tactical fighter-bombers that equip most USAF wings, the B-52H is not dependent upon having useable air bases at a sufficient range from combat zones, given that those bases are often subject to political whims. In terms of targets destroyed, rather than merely missions flown, its combat performance has always been exemplary. As a direct result of this, in 2024, the USAF planned to keep a fleet of 62 B-52Hs operational until at least 2044, when the estimated 32,000 to 37,000 flight hours fatigue life of the flexing upper wing surfaces will elapse. However, replacement of the upper wing skins and other local repairs could still add a further ten years to the veteran's service life.

## CHAPTER SIX  READY FOR THE FUTURE

Attrition accounted for 11 B-52Hs between 1967 and 2015. Twelve more were withdrawn and not upgraded and four were consigned to use as ground instructional airframes. However, ten are maintained in long-term storage with the 309th Aerospace Maintenance and Regeneration Group (AMARG) at Davis-Monthan AFB, Arizona, for potential use as replacements or additions to the frontline fleet. So far, two (60-0034, reassigned to Barksdale in May 2019, and 61-0007 for the 69th BS at Minot in 2016) have been resurrected. The latter aircraft had been in storage for eight years before undergoing regeneration and many updates at the Oklahoma City Air Logistics Complex. 60-0034, assigned to the 23rd BS, made an important visit to Indonesia in June 2023 to explore cooperation with local forces in the light of increasing tensions in the area.

The biggest improvement is likely to come from the long-discussed replacement of the aircraft's eight Pratt & Whitney TF33 turbofan engines with eight Rolls-Royce BR725/F130 digitally-controlled turbofans, greatly increasing fuel efficiency and range. New pylons and nacelles will also be needed for the eight F130s, which will be assembled at the Allison engine plant in the USA. Re-engining has been the subject of many committee meetings since 1996, as B-52H operators became increasingly aware that the last new TF33 engine was delivered in 1985. Some rejected proposals called for four very powerful turbofans to reduce fuel costs. From 2002, when the prospect of retirement of the B-52H receded to an unspecified date around 2040, the economics of engine renewal became more attractive.

B-52Hs have also been used in experiments with blended synthetic fuels, but the venerable bomber with TF33 engines burns 3334 gallons of fuel per hour, whatever its composition. F130s offer 20 per cent better fuel economy. With new engines and other improvements, the Stratofortress will certainly be the most enduring of the six heavy bombers that the USAF has developed prior to the B-21 Raider, which is due to enter service in 2027.

B-52H-145-BW 60-0036 *TAGBOARD FLYER* of the 419th FTS returns to Edwards AFB with an AGM-183A ARRW dummy round attached to its port underwing inner pylon at the completion of the weapon's first captive-carry flight on 12 June 2019 (*USAF*)

# APPENDICES

# COLOUR PLATES COMMENTARY

## 1
### B-52H-135-BW 60-0001 *Memphis Belle IV* of the 20th BS/2nd BW, Barksdale AFB, Louisiana, 1996

This was the first B-52H, delivered on 9 May 1961 to the 379th BW at Wurtsmith AFB, Michigan. The aircraft was named in honour of World War 2 B-17F 41-24485, the first of its kind to complete 25 missions. *Memphis Belle III* was B-52G 59-2594, while the second aircraft in the series was Maj Buddy Jones' *Rolling Thunder* 355th TFW F-105D Thunderchief fighter-bomber, *Memphis Belle II*. 60-0001 currently serves with the 2nd BW's 96th BS.

## 2
### B-52H-165-BW 61-0006 *OLD SOLDIER II* of the 11th BS/2nd BW, Diego Garcia, December 1998

B-52Hs adopted tail codes after SAC was replaced by ACC in 1992. 'LA' indicates 'Louisiana', while the more obvious 'BD' for Barksdale is used by AFRC's 93rd BS. From March 2009 the 11th BS aircraft were transferred to the 93rd BS, but this example moved to the 96th BS, with whom it still serves in 2025. Nicknamed *OLD SOLDIER II* and adorned with Gen Douglas MacArthur-inspired nose art, 61-0006 is depicted here whilst still serving with the 11th BS during the aircraft's commitment to Operation *Desert Fox*.

## 3
### B-52H-135-BW 60-0011 of the 11th BS/2nd BW, Barksdale AFB, Louisiana, March 1999

As flagship of the 11th BS, this B-52H featured the squadron's tail markings and 'Mr Jiggs' squadron nose art, which originated in 1918. The appropriately numbered 60-0011 was used by the B-52 Formal Training Unit at Barksdale prior to its deployment to Fairford as a replacement aircraft in March 1999 for OAF, eventually acquiring five CALCM launch score markings following service in the latter campaign. 60-0011 continues to serve as the unit commander's aircraft in 2025.

## 4
### B-52H-155-BW 60-0051 *APPETITE FOR DESTRUCTION II* of the 23rd BS/5th BW, RAF Fairford, Gloucestershire, March 1999

With a fearsome steel shark artwork echoing its name, this B-52H was a CALCM-launching replacement aircraft among five Stratofortresses sent from Minot to Fairford for OAF. Missions flown by 60-0051 would be denoted by bomb tally markings next to the panel that contained the crew's names. B-52Hs from both Minot and Barksdale usually feature the crew names on the forward fuselage within an outline map of North Dakota and Louisiana, respectively. This aircraft is presently assigned to the 93rd BS at Barksdale.

## 5
### B-52H-170-BW 61-0016 *Free Bird/POW-MIA REMEMBER* of the 11th BS/2nd BW, RAF Fairford, Gloucestershire, April 1999

Although christened *Free Bird*, 61-0016 was actually nicknamed 'First Strike' following its participation in the first wave of CALCM launches in *Noble Anvil* (OAF) – the bomber had first appeared at Fairford on 17 February 1999. It was among the aircraft that were 'de-nuclearised' under the START treaty, after which it was moved to the 20th BS. 61-0016 displayed 12 CALCM 'scores' and a POW-MIA emblem, recalling the captured flyers of Vietnam and later conflicts. The aircraft is presently assigned to the 96th BS.

## 6
### B-52H-160-BW 60-0062 *CAJUN FEAR* of the 20th BS/2nd BW, RAF Fairford, Gloucestershire, April 1999

This was one of the two replacement aircraft (including 60-0049) that arrived at Fairford from Barksdale bearing, and equipped to launch, AGM-142 Have Nap missiles. It retained nuclear capability, and had first flown in that role with the 4239th Strategic Wing at Kincheloe AFB, Michigan, from January 1962. Still proudly wearing its *CAJUN FEAR* artwork, 60-0062 currently flies with the 23rd BS.

## 7
### B-52H-145-BW 60-0033 *INSTRUMENT OF DESTRUCTION* of the 23rd BS/5th BW, RAF Fairford, Gloucestershire, May 1999

This B-52H completed 13 OAF missions from Fairford as a rotational replacement aircraft. It displayed some unusually elaborate nose-art on its overall FS36118 Gunship Gray paintwork. The aircraft also flew numerous missions from Andersen AFB with the 69th BS (with whom it still serves) during OEF and OIF I.

## 8
### B-52H-140-BW 60-0020 *"The Mad Bolshevik"* of the 20th BS/2nd BW, RAF Fairford, Gloucestershire, June 1999

Displaying impressive CALCM and bomb scoreboards either side of the Louisiana-shaped crew name panel, 60-0020 was the 20th BS's flagship during OAF. It was also amongst the first eight B-52Hs to appear at Fairford, on 17 February 1999, for the impending campaign. The 'Mad Bolshevik' nose art dates back to the squadron's origins in 1917. This bomber was placed in storage at AMARG in 2008 as AABC0485 for potential future revival.

## 9
### B-52H-140-BW 61-0008 *NYPD WE REMEMBER 11 SEPT 01* of the 93rd BS/917th Wing, Al Udeid AB, Qatar, December 2001

Decorated with the 917th Wing badge and crew names in an arrow-head outline (inspired by the 93rd BS's insignia), this B-52H was one of many US military aircraft at the time honouring the memories of those killed in the '9/11' attack on the World Trade Center. Formerly known as *Darth Gator*, the bomber had been transferred to the 93rd BS (with whom it remains in 2025) from the 7th BW.

## 10
### B-52H-170-BW 61-0022 *NYPD WE REMEMBER 11 SEPT 01* of the 93rd BS/917th Wing, Diego Garcia, 2002–04

Bearing titling beneath the cockpit that was identical to that seen on 61-0008, but with *NYPD* in white, this B-52H flew many combat missions from Diego Garcia during OEF and OIF I before eventually being retired and sent to Sheppard AFB, Texas, in September 2009 as a GB-52H instructional airframe. The aircraft had a different NYPD '9/11' marking beneath the cockpit on its right side.

## 11
### B-52H-175-BW 61-0029 *SAC TIME* of the 93rd BS/917th Wing, Barksdale AFB, Louisiana, 2004

With nose art harking back to the pre-1992 era of SAC, with whom this aircraft flew for 30 years with ten different bomb wings, *SAC TIME* was adorned with 17 'Indian Outlaws' tomahawk mission markings during OIF I – these were removed prior to the aircraft returning to Barksdale, however. Previously known as *Renegade* with the 5th BW, 61-0029 had its *SAC TIME* artwork replaced by markings to commemorate the 93rd BS's 100th anniversary in 2017. The bomber is presently the unit CO's jet.

## 12
### B-52H-175-BW 61-0031 *JUDGMENT DAY* of the 93rd BS/917th Wing, Barksdale AFB, Louisiana, December 2014

An OAF participant, this B-52H was amongst the first eight Barksdale aircraft to arrive at Fairford on 17 February 1999 as part of the 20th EBS/2nd AEG, serving alongside B-1Bs and KC-135s at the Gloucestershire base. Subsequently reassigned to the AFRC-manned 93rd BS (with whom it still serves in 2025), the aircraft had the name *COMMANDER MAXWELL "MAX" MATLOCK* applied beneath the cockpit on its left side after ten-year-old cancer sufferer 'Max' Matlock became the bomber's honorary crew chief. The distinctive *JUDGMENT DAY* artwork has been applied to 61-0031 in several styles over the years.

## 13
### B-52H-145-BW 60-0025 *OL' CROW Express II* of the 20th BS/2nd BW, Al Udeid AB, Qatar, April 2016

This combat veteran flew in *Desert Strike* (as an air spare) in September 1996 and launched CALCMs in *Desert Fox* two years later. At Al Udeid, it contributed to OIF I from April 2003 and the assault on IS from April 2016, adding to its scoreboard of 45 bombing missions and a CALCM launch. Still assigned to the 20th in 2025, 60-0025, along with 60-0028, made a BTF deployment to Diego Garcia from 22 March through to 2 April 2024.

## 14
### B-52H-170-BW 61-0020 *The Big Stick* of the 20th BS/2nd BW, Barksdale AFB, Louisiana, June 2017

This aircraft has served as the flagship of the 20th BS for a number of years, the bomber featuring a tail code and unit designation with white drop shadows as is traditional for such an aircraft in the USAF. Its groundcrew also kept a detailed scoreboard of its many missions beneath the 20th BS insignia. The veteran bomber's first taste of combat came during *Desert Fox*, followed by OAF, when it was sent to Fairford as a replacement B-52H.

## 15
### B-52H-160-BW 60-0060 *IRON Butterfly* of the 23rd BS/5th BW, RAAF Base Darwin, May 2019

A participant in the opening CALCM barrage of OIF I on 21 March 2003, this B-52H, as 'Dogleg 25', fired all eight of its missiles at targets in the Baghdad area. Commanded by Capt Jason Horton, with Capt Patrick McDonald (who dropped the B-52's first LGB in April 2003) as navigator, the aircraft completed a 16.1-hour mission. In March 2019, 60-0060 was one of two B-52Hs from the 23rd BS that were sent to RAAF Base Darwin from Andersen AFB for Exercise *Diamond Shield*. The aircraft is still assigned to the 23rd BS in 2025.

## 16
### B-52H-150-BW 60-0037 *WHAM BAM II* of the 69th EBS/5th BW, Andersen AFB, Guam, July 2019

Previously nicknamed *Black Widow*, this aircraft participated in OAF with the 96th EBS as a replacement B-52H, routinely operated from Guam whilst forward-deployed and flew from Al Udeid in April 2021 during the final stages of OEF. On 20 May 2024 two 5th BW B-52Hs (60-0037 and 61-0018) arrived at Fairford for BTF-Europe 24-3. Operating with the 69th EBS, they conducted interoperability exercises with other NATO partners.

## 17
### B-52H-150-BW 60-0044 *EXCALIBUR* 23rd BS/5th BW, RAF Fairford, Gloucestershire, September 2020

Deployed to Diego Garcia for *Desert Fox* and to Fairford for OAF, this aircraft also visited Darwin on 8 December 2014 while operating from Andersen AFB. It has routinely flown from Fairford since 1999, using the 'Hyla' callsign in October 2022 for inter-operations with Turkish and Swedish air force units. 60-0044's nickname and artwork was applied while the bomber was assigned to Lt Col Robert Bender, CO of the Minot-based 5th Operations Support Squadron in 2004.

## 18
### B-52H-175-BW 61-0039 *THE WARRIOR* of the 69th BS/5th BW, Minot AFB, North Dakota, 2021

This aircraft, the penultimate B-52H built, was a visitor to Fairford as one of the five Minot bombers that were replacements rotated into the base for OAF in 1999. It was also involved in OEF two years later. Its assignment to the 5th BW commenced in July 1991, and the veteran bomber remains with the wing some 34 years later.

## 19
### B-52H-165-BW 61-0010 *JUNKYARD DOG* of the 20th BS/2nd BW, Barksdale AFB, Louisiana, July 2021

This B-52H was one of seven deployed to Fairford in October 1998 for the 16th AEW in a successful attempt to persuade the Yugoslav leadership to sign a ceasefire. It presently serves as the 343rd BS flagship (hence the stylised tail codes and *343rd BS* titling), and attended the Royal International Air Tattoo at Fairford in July 2024.

## 20
### B-52H-160-BW 60-0059 *THE DEVIL'S OWN* of the 96th BS/2nd BW, Barksdale AFB, Louisiana, 2022

This aircraft was the 96th BS's flagship (a role it has performed since the 1990s) in April 2022 when Lt Col Vanessa Wilcox became the first female B-52 squadron commander. She was a Weapons Systems Officer prior to becoming CO of the squadron and inscribing her name on 60-0059. The squadron's 'Devil and bomb' insignia dates back to World War 1. The 96th EBS pioneered continuous bomber presence deployments to Guam from 2004 to 2011, with this aircraft participating in a number of these operations.

## 21
### B-52H-165-BW 61-0003 *OLD IRONSIDES III* of the 69th BS/5th BW, RAF Fairford, Gloucestershire, April 2023

This aircraft was the 5th BW's flagship for a BTF deployment to Guam in June 2010, and it was also a visitor to Fairford in February 2022. During a mission from the latter base, it was escorted over Iceland by Portuguese Air Force F-16AMs and RAF Typhoons. The bomber has served with ten different wings during its many years of service, including a previous spell with the 5th BW between 1970–74, attracting several nicknames including *Miss Behavin*, *Dragon Slayer* and *Buff Bunny*.

## 22
### B-52H-170-BW 61-0015 *The Last Laugh* of the 96th EBS/2nd BW, Andersen AFB, Guam, March–July 2023

Emphasising the USAF's global strike power, this aircraft flew several sorties with the Republic of China Air Force during a BTF deployment to Guam that ran from March to July 2023. During a previous visit to Andersen AFB, 61-0015 had appeared at the Australian International Airshow at Avalon Airport on 25 February 2015 whilst participating in Exercise *Cope North 15*.

Training for B-52H crew can involve visits to *Red Flag* exercises or, in this case, a Weapons School Integration exercise – both events staged at Nellis AFB. With Las Vegas shimmering in the background, 93rd BS B-52H-175-BW 61-0029 departs Nellis on 2 June 2021 (*USAF*)

B-52H-155-BW 60-0050 *DRAGON'S INFERNO* of the 419th FTS is the AFFTC's longest-serving flight test aircraft, having first arrived at Edwards AFB in August 1985. Since then, it has contributed to numerous programmes, including the Boeing X-51 Waverider hypersonic vehicle and synthetic fuel trials. Seen here in December 2004, it has Edwards' distinctive 'ED' codes on its large fin. More recently, 60-0050 and sister-aircraft 60-0036 tested the AGM-183A ARRW and the Bomber Modular Acquisition System data management network (*USAF*)

# INDEX

Page numbers in **bold** refer to illustration and their captions.

Afghanistan 52, 55–70, **57**, **62**, **69**, **70**, 71, 78, 82
Air Expeditionary Forces (AEFs) 13
Air Force Space Command 27
al-Qaeda 55, 58, 61–62, 63, 66–69
Anderson, Maj Keith 20
armament 7–8, 48–54, **48**, **49**, **50**, **52**, **53**, **54**, 77, 77–79, 88, 91, 92

B-2A 8
B-52G 7, 8, 14–15
B-52H **6**, 7, 7–8, 8, 9–10, 13
　60-0001 *Memphis Belle IV* **6**, **1**(**33**, 93), **44**
　60-0002 *SPIRIT OF BOSSIER & SHREVEPORT* **7**, **69**
　60-0003: **18**
　60-0011: **11**, **3**(**34**, 93), **44**, **48**
　60-0014 'Duke 02' 16–18
　60-0019: **71**
　60-0020 *The Mad Bolshevik* **25**, 30, **8**(**36**, 93), **44**
　60-0025 *OL' CROW Express II* **13**(**39**, 94), **45**, 80
　60-0026: **8**
　60-0032: **80**
　60-0033 *INSTRUMENT OF DESTRUCTION* **7**(**36**, 93), **44**
　60-0036 *TAGBOARD FLYER* **92**
　60-0037 *WHAM BAM II* **16**(**40**, 94), **45**, 85
　60-0044 *EXCALIBUR* **17**(**41**, 94), **45**, 87
　60-0049: 12, 30, **32**
　60-0050 *DRAGON'S INFERNO* **50**, 89, 90–91, **95**
　60-0051 *APPETITE FOR DESTRUCTION II* **27**, **4**(**34**, 93), **44**, **76**
　60-0054 'Duke 01' 10, 16–18
　60-0054 *MUD BUFF* **14**
　60-0059 *THE DEVIL'S OWN* 11, **12**, **23**, **20**(**42**, 94), **45**, **55**
　60-0060 *IRON Butterfly* **15**(**40**, 94), **45**, **72**
　60-0062 *CAJUN FEAR* 30, **30**, **6**(**35**, 93), **44**
　61-0002 *Eagle's Wrath III* **29**, 30
　61-0003 *OLD IRONSIDES III* **21**(**43**, 95), **45**, 85, 87
　61-0004: **69**
　61-0006 *OLD SOLDIER II* **2**(**33**, 93), **44**
　61-0008 *NYPD WE REMEMBER 11 SEPT 01*: **9**(**37**, 93), 47, 85
　61-0010 *JUNKYARD DOG* **19**(**42**, 94), **45**
　61-0013 *HIGH TENSION III* **84**
　61-0015 *The Last Laugh* **22**(**43**, 95), **45**, 86
　61-0016 *Free Bird/POW-MIA REMEMBER* **5**(**35**, 93), **44**
　61-0020 *The Big Stick* **14**(**39**, 94), **45**
　61-0022 *NYPD WE REMEMBER 11 SEPT 01*: **10**(**37**, 93–94), **44**, 47
　61-0029 *SAC TIME* **11**(**38**, 94), **44**, **95**
　61-0031 *JUDGMENT DAY* **12**(**38**, 94), **45**
　61-0039 *THE WARRIOR* **18**(**41**, 94), **45**, **47**
bomb-bay **51**
Bomber Vector programme 9
bombs 9, 11, 15, **28**, 29, 30, 31, 32, 47, 48, **48**, 50–52, **50**, **52**, **53**, 54, **54**, 57–58, 58, 59, 61, 62–63, **62**, 64, 67, 68–69, **69**, 76, 77, 78, 79, **79**, 80, 81, **81**, 82, **82**, 83, **84**, 90
Brooks, Col William 11
Buchanan, Maj Gen Walter 60

Campbell, Lt Col Don 49
Carpenter, Col Floyd L **14**, 16, **16**, 27, 31, 49, 74, 75
carpet bombing 46, 60, 64
Clark, Gen Wesley 31, 47
close air support (CAS) 15
cluster munitions 52, 78
Cole, Gen George P 11
combat configuration 9–10
Combat Network Communication Technology (CONECT) system 81
*Combat Round Robin* missions 29

Combined Air Interdiction of Fielded Forces policy 46
CONECT system 88
Continuous Bomber Presence (CBP) 86
cruise missiles 8, 9, 13, 20, **20**, 21, 24, **25**, 27–28, **27**, 28–29, 30, 48, **48**, 49, **49**, 52, **72**, 73–74, 74–75
Cuban Missile Crisis 6

Effects Based Targeting 72
electronic countermeasures (ECM) 18, 31, **70**, 88–89
11 September 2001 terrorist attacks 22, 55, 71
exercises 11, 25, 85, 86–88, 90, **90**

flaps **15**
flexible targeting 61–62, 64, 67, 77
formations
　2nd AEG 18–19, 20, **26**, 31
　2nd BW 6, 10–11, 16, 19, **21**, **25**, **26**, 30, 32, **1**–**3**(**33**–**34**, 93), **3**(**34**, 93), **5**–**6**(**35**, 93), **8**(**36**, 93), **13**–**14**(**39**, 94), **19**–**20**(**42**, 94), **22**(**43**, 95), 54, 58, **70**, 74, 80, 85, 85–86, 86–87, 91
　5th BW 6, 10, 12, 26, **26**, 29–30, **4**(**34**, 93), **7**(**36**, 93), **15**(**40**, 94), **16**(**40**, 94), **17**–**18**(**41**, 94), **21**(**43**, 95), 47, 56, **69**, 79, 85, 86, 86–87, 87
　11th BS 11, **11**, 26, **2**(**33**, 93), **3**(**34**, 93), **5**(**35**, 93), **48**
　20th BS 11, 20, **25**, 26, 27, **28**, 30, **1**(**33**, 93), **6**(**35**, 93), **8**(**36**, 93), **13**–**14**(**39**, 94), **19**(**42**, 94), 54, 58, 74, 79, 80
　20th EBS 27, 32, 69
　23rd BS 12, 19, 20, 26, 29–30, **4**(**34**, 93), **7**(**36**, 93), **15**(**40**, 94), **17**(**41**, 94), **69**, 70, **72**, 74, 75–76, **76**, **81**, 83, 84, 85–86, 87, 92
　23rd EBS 85
　28th BW 18–19, 31, 87
　34th EBS 57, 83–84
　40th AEW 56, **57**, 69, **71**, 73, 74, 79
　49th TES 12, 52, 90
　69th BS **21**(**43**, 95), **47**, 83, 87–88
　69th EBS 9, **16**(**40**, 94), **18**(**41**, 94), 70, **83**, 84, **84**, 87, 92
　92nd BW 10, 85
　93rd BS 6, 11, **18**, **9**–**12**(**37**–**38**, 93-94), 47, 52, 65, 77, **95**
　96th BS 11, **12**, 16–18, 20, **23**, **20**(**42**, 94), **55**, 56, 74, **80**
　96th EBS 19, **22**, **22**(**43**, 95), 81
　184th BW **18**
　305th AMW **22**
　307th BW/OG 11–12
　319th BW **8**
　410th BW 10, 85
　419th FTS 50, **50**, 87, 91, **92**, **95**
　449th BW **7**
　457th AEG 77, 78
　509th BW 8, 87
　719th BS **7**
　917th BW **18**
　917th Wing 11–12, **9**–**12**(**37**–**38**, 93-94), 58, 74
Forward Air Controllers 57, 60, 62
Franks, Gen Tommy 56
FRY air defences 32
funding 13

Global Power missions 13
Global Strike Command 12
Goossen, Lt Col Paul 84
Griffin, Col Wendell 19

Harris, Adm Harry B 86
Hawkins, Col James A 11
Haynor, Lt Col Douglas 20
Hornberg, Maj Gen Hal 24

in-flight refuelling 10, 15, 16–17, 26, 27, 31, 57, **59**, **69**, 76, **82**

Islamic State 54, 79–84

Joint Surveillance Target Attack Radar System 75, 76–77, 79, 88
Jumper, Gen John 58, 78

Kay, David 22
Keck, Lt Gen Thomas J 47

Leaptrott, Lt Col Timothy 31

MacKay Trophy 18
McPeak, Gen Merrill 7
MILSTAR satellite network 78
missiles 7, 9, 13, 15, 17, 21, **21**, **25**, 30, **30**, 32, 49–50, 54, **72**, 74, 77, 78

NATO 23–24, 25, 26, 30, 46, 47, 85, 86–87
New Strategic Arms Reduction Treaty programme 8
nocturnal missions 63–64
Northrop Grumman B-2A Spirit 7, 31, 74
nose-art **11**, **44**–**45**, 47, **48**

Offensive Avionics System upgrades, 2000: 88
operating costs 13
Operation *Allied Force* 20, 23, **23**, 25–31, **25**, **26**, **27**, **28**, **29**, **30**, 75
Operation *Anaconda* **55**, 68–69, 70
Operation *Arrow* 46
Operation *Deliberate Force* 23, 24–25, 27, 32
Operation *Deny Flight* 24, 56
Operation *Desert Fox* 19, 19–22, **20**, **21**, **22**, 49, 56
Operation *Desert Storm* 12, 14–15, 63, 71, 72, 74, 78
Operation *Desert Strike* 14, 16–18, 21, 48
Operation *Desert Thunder* 18–19, **18**, 19
Operation *Inherent Resolve* 79–84, **80**, **81**, **82**, **83**, **84**, 88
Operation *Iraqi Freedom* I 12, 71–79, **71**, **72**, **76**, 79
Operation *Jagged Knife* 70, 82
Owen, Col Robert C 24

performance 10, 13, 91
presence patrols 87
Project *Quick Start* **32**
Project *Seek Eagle* 77
Project *Straight Pin* 7

quick reaction team air strikes 82

Rockwell B-1B Lancer, B-1B 7, **18**, 21, 31, 46, 47, 57, **57**, 58, 59, 60, 64, 65, 66, 68, 70, 75, 80, 83–84

service 6–7, 91
Shelton, Gen Henry 30, 47
Shock and Awe strikes 76
Syria 54, 79, 80, 83

targeting pods 9, 12, 21, **32**, 52–53, 77, 87, 89, **89**, 91
targeting system 89–90
targets of opportunity 61, 77
Total Force Enterprise (TFE) 11–12

Ukraine 54, 87
upgrades 7–8, 88–92
US Marine Corps 31, 58, 63, 69, 82
US Navy 29, 58, 61, 64, 67, 74, 75
USAF Weapons School 52

Wind-Corrected Munitions Dispenser (WCMD) 53–54

X-51 Waverider hypersonic vehicle 90–91, **95**

Yugoslavia, break up of 23–32, 46–47